ECCE ROMANI

Student's Companion 2

Prepared by The Scottish Classics Group

Oliver & Boyd

Teacher's Notes

The *Student's Companions* are not courses in their own right. As their name suggests, their primary purpose is to supplement the *Ecce Romani* course books and to make available in accessible form the sort of material which Latin teachers have always used to exemplify the general educational value of Latin study. *Student's Companion Book 2* is designed specifically to supplement *Ecce Romani* Books 3–5. Each unit of study is linked very closely with the grammatical and vocabulary input of the chapters of *Ecce Romani* to which it is related.

When deciding which words to give at the end of exercises/unseens/ comprehensions, we have assumed that the pupils have already tackled the chapters of the main course to which the specific Unit refers. All words are listed in the main vocabulary except those new words which are given at the end of exercises but do not appear again in the book. Most of the material in the *Companion Books*, therefore, could profitably be used even by pupils who are using other course books.

One obvious use for the *Companions* would be as homework exercises. Equally, parts could be used as extension material for more able pupils while the teacher gives additional practice to those who have not completely grasped certain linguistic points in the main course. It would be a pity, however, if their use was limited to such pupils; for they contain material which is intrinsically important for all pupils. Indeed, those who are struggling with the linguistic content of the course may find parts of the *Companion* easier to tackle than the main course itself.

It will be for the teacher to decide how much or how little of the material to use, depending upon the amount of time available and on the ability of the pupils. It is likely that most advantage will be derived if the *Companions* are used flexibly to meet the needs of the moment, rather than slavishly followed from cover to cover.

Within each Unit there are five main sections:

(a) **Exercenda**: These contain a wide variety of Latin exercises designed to reinforce the grammatical input of the Unit. When devising the main course, we had to strike a balance between providing teachers with all the exercises they might need and discouraging the pupils by confronting them with very thick textbooks.

One regular feature in all **Exercenda** units in *Companion Book* 2 is the Comprehension/Interpretation passage. For some time now, it has been recognised that one of the essential steps towards translating a passage of Latin is to encourage pupils to get an initial overall impression of what it says. In each unit of *Companion Book* 2, there are continuous passages upon which a series of questions is asked. These questions are in two main categories. Firstly, there are straightforward comprehension questions which test whether the pupils have grasped the main points in the story. However, this type of question can often result in a mechanical exercise which is much less demanding than translation. In the "Discussion Points", therefore, we have tried to introduce higher-level interpretation skills. For example, pupils have to "read between the lines" in some way and give their own reactions to what the author is saying — a small, but significant step towards literary criticism.

Only some of the questions are suitable for examination purposes. Others may not be suitable since they rely on information which is not immediately available in the passage. Frequently, there will not be only one correct answer, and the value of the questions will lie in the sharing of ideas which can come from class discussion.

It will be noted that the Atalanta story appeared as part of the "Additional Reading or Test Material" in *Teacher's Book* 3. In Unit X, an alternative version, incorporating additional parts of the story as told by Ovid in *Metamorphoses X*, is offered for comprehension/interpretation.

(b) **Derivanda**: In the Teacher's Books, we have constantly encouraged teachers to devote time to showing how frequently English words can be traced back to Latin. The importance of this sort of work is being increasingly recognised in the campaign to increase literacy among pupils. The exercises provided are far from exhaustive, but it is hoped that they will prove useful to the hard-pressed teacher who cannot always devote as much time as he/she would like to this aspect of Latin teaching. These exercises should be particularly valuable in helping pupils to realise that there are patterns into which derivatives fall.

Although many of the exercises are laid out in matrix form, it is not essential that all the columns be completed in writing. The format is designed to guide the pupils' thinking. Certainly, we would expect pupils to consult their English dictionaries regularly, but it will probably be more beneficial to use what they find there as a basis for class discussion rather than as a mechanical copying exercise.

(c) **Memoranda**: These consist of Latin mottoes, sayings, poetry, songs, etc., drawn from a wide variety of sources. Besides helping to reinforce the pupils' grasp of the Latin language, these should give them a wealth of wise and pithy sayings on which to ponder. The aim is to help pupils realise that Latin is not "dead" but is to be found all around them.

The sources quoted are many and varied, and there are some which we have been unable to trace exactly. For reasons of space and consistency, therefore, we have not provided a list of exact references but have given only a summary reference in the text. However, should any reader wish to have a list of the available references, these can be obtained on application to the authors through the publishers.

(d) **Miranda**: interesting "survivals" from Roman times. A questioning rather than a passive attitude to life is something that is to be encouraged in our young people. These sections try to show pupils that curiosity about our customs and usages can be fascinating and enjoyable, as well as useful. The sections are by no means definitive as far as content is concerned. In fact, each **Miranda** section only scratches the surface of the information available on the topic. However, the hope is that at least some of them may spark off a new interest which pupils may wish to pursue in more detail for themselves.

(e) **Aenigmata**: Puzzles of various kinds are used to provide revision exercises in language and background.

Although some of the words/phrases listed in the Appendices have already appeared in the *Companion Books*, it was felt that pupils would appreciate having all of these brought together for handy reference.

In addition to the Units, there are grammatical tables which bring together the accidence introduced throughout the course. Teachers have rightly pointed out that pupils sometimes forget these tables when the particular course book which contains them has been withdrawn from use. The syntactical rules are not included, since it is assumed that the course books will be available to pupils at the times when they are using these additional exercises for practice. However, if a reference book is required, *The Latin Language (A Handbook for Students)* (published separately) provides a description of all the syntax which is likely to be required at school level.

Finally, it is hoped that the plans for making models will not only give pupils pleasure, but will also make them think a little more deeply about what they are doing/making. Because the plans are for "working" models, it has been recommended that they be constructed in wood; but it may be possible to create them in card if only a battle scene is required. No measurements are given since these war machines came in all shapes and sizes, but the builder can design his/her own model from the basic drawings provided. Pupils should be warned to exercise great care when operating these working models. The twisted cord, in particular, can produce a very powerful spring.

Acknowledgements

We are grateful to the following for supplying photographs and giving permission for their use: Heather Angel (p. 65); Colchester and Essex Museum (p. 57); Edinburgh Royal Choral Union (p. 90); The Mansell Collection (pp. 15, 22, 27, 28, 29, 47, 50, 93); Christine Osborne Pictures (p. 37); Post Office Letters (p. 78); The Yorkshire Museum (p. 58).

Contents

Unit IX (Chapters 28–32)

Exercenda

1 *Responde Latine:*
(These questions are based on Chapters 31 and 32.)

    (a) quot lecti circum mensam positi sunt?

    (b) cur convivae mappas secum portabant?

    (c) ubi convivae convenerunt, intraveruntne statim in triclinium?

    (d) postquam omnes in lectis accubuerunt, quid primum in triclinium portatum est?

    (e) dum gustatio editur, quid faciunt convivae?

    (f) cur sero ad cenam venit Titus?

    (g) ubi servi cibum ad mensam portaverunt, quid Tito dare iussi sunt?

    (h) cur cena laudata est?·

    (i) cur coquus vocatus est?

    (j) postquam convivae frusta aut porci aut pullorum ederunt, quo fercula ablata sunt?

2 *Select and translate:*

    (a) incolae, _____ in insula habitabant, liberos servare non poterant.   qui/quae/quos

    (b) liberi, _____ in tertio tabulato Cornelia vidit, se servare non poterant.   qui/quae/quos

    (c) convivae laudaverunt cibum _____ servi in triclinium portabant.   qui/quem/quam

    (d) convivae, _____ servi cibum dederunt, coquum laudaverunt.   cui/qui/quibus

(e) Titus, _____ frater est Cornelius, sero ad cenam venit.   qui/quem/cuius

(f) audivistine eam fabulam, _____ de Pseudolo narrata est?   qui/quae/quam

(g) cives valde timebant incendia, _____ saepe in urbe videbant.   qui/quae/quod

(h) servi, a _____ cibus allatus erat, iam defessi erant.   qui/quo/quibus

3 *Translate:*

    (a) illa puella est filia illius senatoris.

    (b) ego ad Curiam ibo, illa domum redibit.

    (c) da illa frusta pullorum eis servis.

    (d) soleae eorum a servis ablatae sunt.

    (e) "cuius est ille pinguis porcus?" rogavit Aurelia.

    (f) ubi Titus advenit, frater nihil ei dixit.

    (g) ei servi eam ad illam domum lectica ferunt.

    (h) illa domina est valde irata quod ancilla crines neglegenter pectit.

4 *Translate:*

    (a) is servus, qui a fundo effugit, a vilico punietur.

    (b) equi ab auriga ferociter agebantur.

    (c) miles gladio necatus est.

    (d) bona ab incolis per insulae fenestras coniecta sunt.

    (e) cistae e villa portabuntur et in raeda ponentur.

    (f) quot amici a senatore salutabantur?

    (g) cena optima a coquo parata erat.

    (h) puellae flammis et fumo oppressae erant.

    (i) ova, quae convivis dantur, abhinc tres dies in urbe empta sunt.

    (j) quod amici quidam ad cenam invitati sunt, multa ab Aurelia in urbe ementur.

    (k) in triclinium duceris et a convivis laudaberis.

5 *Translate:*

    (a) convivae cena delectati coquum laudaverunt.

    (b) Aulus a caupone scelesto necatus ab amico inventus est.

    (c) multae epistolae a Cornelio scriptae ad amicos missae sunt.

    (d) cibus in ferculis positus in triclinium latus est.

    (e) porcus bene coctus in frusta scissus est.

    (f) bona incolarum e fenestra eiecta ab amicis servata sunt.

    (g) raeda e fossa extracta ad cauponam agebatur.

    (h) caro in culina parata ad mensam nunc portabitur.

(a) The Lion and the Mouse

olim leo quidam in silva dormiebat cum subito trans corpus eius mus
transcurrit.   leo ex somno excitatus murem devorare parabat.   mus
tamen perterritus "noli" inquit "me necare!   ego numquam te
vulneravi.   fortasse te olim servare potero."
5   risit leo: "quomodo tu, qui es tam parvus, tam infirmus, me
servare poteris?   ego enim maximus atque potentissimus sum.
ego sum omnium animalium rex."   sed quamquam haec dixit, leo
tandem lacrimis commotus (videbatur enim ille mus tam parvus et
innocens esse), eum effugere sivit.
10   post paucos dies idem leo, cibum in silva petens, in laqueum
incidit.   voce magna clamabat, nam se ex laqueo liberare non
poterat.   tota silva clamoribus eius resonabat.
      mus ille autem, cum clamorem audivisset, vocem agnovit leonis
qui eum effugere siverat.   ad locum igitur celeriter accurrit.   mox
15 dentibus nodos rodebat; ita leo e laqueo liberatus est.   potentissima
saepe sunt etiam parva animalia.

potentissimus, -a, -um, very powerful	**resono** (1), to resound
rex, regis (*m*), king	**agnosco** (3), **agnovi, agnitum,** to recognise
sino (3), **sivi, situm,** to allow	**nodus, -i** (*m*), knot
laqueus, -i (*m*), snare	**rodo** (3), to gnaw

(b) The Mountain and the Mouse

est altera fabula de mure narrata.   mus et mons olim inter se
disputabant.   haec erat disputationis causa: "ego" inquit mons
"magnus et potentissimus sum, sed tu es parvus et infirmus.   cur
igitur tam procax es?"
5   cui respondit mus "cur tu tam gloriosus es?   tu quidem immensus
es.   hoc scio; omnes hoc videre possunt.   at tu, si vis, haec considera!
parvus ego sum, tu magnus.   tu corpus immensum habes, sed
immobile; ego corpus parvum certe habeo, sed valde mobile.   neque
ego omnia facere possum neque tu.   ego silvas ferre non possum, tu
10 ne parvam quidem nucem edere potes."   tum tacebat mons; nihil
enim respondere poterat.

gloriosus, -a, -um, boastful
ne ... quidem, not even
nux, nucis (*f*), nut

7 *Do not translate unless asked to do so, but answer in English the
questions which follow:*

Proserpina is Kidnapped

habitabat in Sicilia dea Ceres, quae flores et arbores et omnes
segetes fovebat.   filiam pulchram habebat, nomine Proserpinam.
mater filiam, filia matrem valde amabat.   cotidie mater et filia
laetae per agros et per silvas una ibant, omnia foventes.
5   olim laeta cum puellis suis errabat Proserpina per agros et
silvas.   ibi inventi sunt flores abundantes, quos simulac conspexit
Proserpina "o puellae," clamavit "accedite et referte mecum sinus
florum plenos!"
mox igitur puellae huc illuc errantes flores varios legebant.
10 undique lecti sunt hyacinthi et croci, lilia alba et rosae, atque multi

alii sine nomine flores.   puellae omnes inter se laetae clamabant,
nam non magnus erat labor.   Proserpina ipsa, dum flores pulchros
legebat, paulatim procul ab amicis carpendi studio ferebatur.   mox
nulla vox puellarum iam procul errantium audiebatur.   Proserpina
15 relicta est sola.

tum illa a Plutone, rege regionis infernae, visa est.   mox puella ab
eo in regna eius abrepta est, semper clamans "eheu, mater!
auferor!   auferor!"   nemo tamen clamores audivit.

brevi tempore ceterae puellae redibant clamantes "Proserpina!
20 Proserpina!   vide flores pulchros quos reportavimus!"   responsum
erat nullum.   Proserpina clamata tacebat.   statim domum
festinaverunt puellae atque rem horrendam Cereri narraverunt.
identidem exclamabat illa "o me miseram!   filia, ubi es?   ubi es,
filia?"   sed Proserpina matrem non audivit.

25 deinde mater, filiam amissam petens, sine fine transcurrebat
omnes terras et omnia maria, neque eam invenire poterat.   interea,
quod omnia a Cerere neglegebantur, florebat nullus flos, nulla
arbor, nulla seges.   tandem mater Solem, qui omnia videt, de filia
abrepta consuluit.   respondit Sol: "ea quam petis in regionibus
30 infernis iam habitat, Plutoni nupta."

Ceres igitur adiit Iovem, regem deorum et fratrem Plutonis.
"cur non punitur" inquit "frater tuus, ille tam scelestus praedo?
quando licebit meae filiae ad terram recedere?   quando dolor meus
finietur?"

35 cui respondit Iuppiter, lacrimis deae motus, "si filia tua, o Ceres,
ieiuna remansit, statim liberabitur; si non, uxor Plutonis erit."

eheu!   sub terra Proserpina tria grana pomi Punici iam ederat.
misera igitur rediit ad terram Ceres sola.   diu domi manebat,
semper dolens neque segetes fovens.   tandem Iuppiter, sollicitus
40 quod iam florebant in terra neque flores neque arbores neque
segetes, Plutonem iussit Proserpinam ad terram remittere.   Cereri
quoque mandata dedit.   "tibi necesse est Proserpinam post sex
menses Plutoni reddere.   posthac omni anno Proserpina sex
menses supra terram, sex menses infra habitabit."

---

flos, floris (*m*), flower
seges, -etis (*f*), crop
foveo, -ere (3), **fovi, fotum,** to
    cherish, care for
sinus, -us (*m*), (curved) arm
lego, -ere (3), **legi, lectum,** to
    gather, pick
paulatim, gradually
carpendi studio, in her
    eagerness to gather
    (the flowers)
infernus, -a, -um, (lying) under
    the earth, of the underworld

amitto, -ere (3), **-misi, -missum,** to
    lose
Sol, Solis (*m*), the Sun
nubo, -ere (3), **nupsi, nuptum**
    (+ *dat*), to wed, marry
rex, regis (*m*), king
dolor, doloris (*m*), grief
ieiunus, -a, -um, without food,
    without eating
tria grana pomi Punici, three
    pomegranate seeds
posthac, after this
annus, -i (*m*), year
mensis, -is (*m*), month

(i) Comprehension questions:

(a) What did Ceres and Proserpina normally do each day?
(b) What did Proserpina do on this particular day?
(c) How did Proserpina become separated from her companions?
(d) Who was Pluto?
(e) Give the prefix and simple verb which combine to produce the compound verb **auferor** (line 18). Translate it.
(f) **nemo tamen clamores audivit** (line 18): Why was this so?
(g) Suggest a natural English translation for the words **Proserpina clamata tacebat** (line 21).
(h) What did Ceres do when she was told that Proserpina had disappeared?
(i) What effect did this have on all living plants?
(j) Why did Ceres go to the Sun for advice?
(k) What was Jupiter's initial reaction? What compromise decision did he finally reach?

(ii) Discussion points:

(a) Besides the meaning given in the vocabulary, the noun **sinus** can also mean "curve", "hollow", "valley", "fold", "bay", "bosom" and "lap". What do all these meanings have in common?
(b) Why do you think Ceres went to Jupiter rather than to another god?
(c) Pick out two words in the text which could be translated "kidnapped". Which do you think is the more descriptive?
(d) Discuss what happened in the third paragraph. Do you feel that the events are natural or contrived? Do you think Ceres could be blamed for what happened to Proserpina? Does the paragraph provide any guidance on the care of children?
(e) Myths tend to be attempts by early people to explain events they do not fully understand. What do you think this myth is trying to explain?

Derivanda

1 *List the Latin words from which these English words are derived and give the meanings of the English words:*

English word	Latin word	Meaning of English word
edible alternative umbrella culinary oval quintet fidelity fable		

2 *From the supines of which Latin verbs are the following derived?*

commotion	addition	scissors
oppression	expectation	pasture

3 *English word families*

(a) **circum** *is often used as a prefix. Find the meanings of these English words:*

circumnavigate   circumscribe   circumspect
circumstantial   circumvent   circumference

(b) *The Latin adjective* **rectus, -a, -um** *is derived from the verb* **regere** *and means literally "drawn in a straight line" (vertically or horizontally). It then comes to mean "upright", "right" or "proper". Find the meanings of:*

rectangle   rectify   erect
rectilinear   rectitude   correct

4 *Latin word families*

It is often possible to deduce the meanings of new Latin words if you already know other words with the same root meaning. You have already met the words printed in bold type in the table below. Deduce the meanings of the other words in the same line:

Noun	Adjective	Adverb	Verb
celeritas	celer	**celeriter**	celero
ferocitas	ferox	**ferociter**	—
rectitudo	rectus	**recte**	rego
neglegentia	neglegens	**neglegenter**	neglego
vigilantia	vigilans	vigilanter	**vigilo**

5 *Use your knowledge of Latin to work out the meanings of these Latin expressions which are commonly used in English:*

(a) The incisor teeth of rodents (rats, squirrels, beavers, **et cetera**) keep growing throughout their lives.
(b) The student had to take a **viva voce** examination as well as a written paper.
(c) The Association Handbook cost members of the public £3 but was supplied **gratis** to members of the Association.
(d) Everyone else had despised his theories, but at last the philosopher recognised in his new colleague an **alter ego** who shared his views.

6 *Use your knowledge of Latin to explain the meanings of the words in bold type:*

(a) You cannot stay long in that **recumbent** position.
(b) Are there any **additives** in this food?
(c) The terrorists placed an **incendiary** device beneath the car.
(d) Some animals are **carnivores**, others **herbivores**.
(e) The pilot of the damaged plane escaped certain death by using the **ejector** seat.

Memoranda

1 The pronouns **is** and **qui** are often used together as follows:

> **is qui**, he who   **ea quae**, she who   **id quod**, that which

e.g.   **is qui** non laborat non manducat.
He who *does not work does not eat.*

id quod est honestum est utile.
What *(that which) is honourable is beneficial.*

Sometimes, for emphasis, the parts of **is, ea, id** come after the relative clause, e.g.

> **qui** non laborat, **is** non manducat.
> **quod** est honestum, **id** est utile.

Frequently in mottoes, the parts of **is, ea, id** are omitted altogether so that **qui** comes to mean "he who" or "people who", and **quod** means "that which" or "what". The forms in which the above mottoes actually appear are

> qui non laborat, non manducat. (St Paul)
> quod honestum utile. (Family motto)

The pronoun **ille, illa, illud** is used in a similar way. For example, Henry III is reported to have said:

> **qui** non dat quod habet, non accipit **ille** quod optat.
> **He who** *does not give what he has, does not receive what he desires.*

Translate the following mottoes which exemplify this idiom:

(a)	non dormit qui custodit.	(James III)
(b)	vincit qui se vincit.	(family motto)
(c)	bis dat qui cito dat.	(Publilius Syrus)
(d)	bis vivit qui bene (vivit).	(family motto)
(e)	qui facit per alium, facit per se.	(legal maxim)
(f)	felix qui potuit rerum cognoscere causas.	(Virgil)
(g)	caelum non animum mutant qui trans mare currunt.	(Horace)
(h)	homines id quod volunt credunt.	(Caesar)
(i)	quod facio valde facio.	(family motto)
(j)	sum quod sum.	(family motto)

vinco (3), to conquer   **vivo** (3), to live
bis, twice   **muto** (1), to change
cito, quickly

2 *The Poverty Trap*

> semper pauper eris, si pauper es, Aemiliane.
>   dantur opes nullis nunc nisi divitibus.
>   Martial, *Epigrams* V.81

opes, opum *(f.pl)*, riches

A Biting Comment!

> Thais habet nigros, niveos Laecania dentes.
> quae ratio est?   emptos haec habet, illa suos.

Martial, Epigrams V.43

niveus, -a, -um, snow-white
dens, dentis (*m*), tooth
ratio, -onis (*f*), reason

You will begin to appreciate something of the rhythm of Latin poetry by reading it aloud. As in every literature, there are different metres in Latin. The two Martial couplets above are examples of the metre called Elegiac Couplet.

The order of the words in Latin poetry may cause difficulty. Sometimes the poet chooses a particular word order to produce a special effect; he has always to fit the words to a rhythmic pattern. This happens in all poetry. For example:

The 100th Psalm: "Him serve with mirth, His praise forth tell",
Tennyson: "On either side the river lie
                            Long fields of barley and of rye."

Miranda   PLACE NAMES

Wherever the Romans went on military expeditions, they were sure to pitch camp. By this they did not mean a casual affair of tents and camp-fires, but something which from the very outset would have a formal shape and at least a ditch and a rampart to define its outline.

Within the Roman army, there were always specialists whose task it was to find and plan the best possible site for camp; and some of the camp sites were so good that what had begun as a temporary camp would often blossom into a fort commanding some key communication point, a river crossing perhaps, or a meeting of natural highways. When the process of conquering an area was complete, the fort might achieve the status of a **colonia** and become a place where soldiers could settle down and become householders and family men.

Many towns in England have names ending in "-caster", "-cester" or "-chester", e.g. Lancaster, Cirencester and Manchester. These usually pinpoint camp sites which developed into towns; but these endings do not directly represent the Latin word **castra**, as is commonly believed. They actually come, in the first instance, from the Old English word *ceaster* ("city" or "fortified place") which in turn was derived from **castra**. The town of Chester had two names: **Deva** and **civitas legionum** ("city of the legions"). This seems to have become *Legaceaster* in Old English, but it was later abbreviated to *Ceaster* to avoid confusion with another town called *Ligoraceaster* (Leicester).

See how many of these Roman camps-turned-towns you can find on a map of England.

Occasionally, the modern name of a town indicates that it had been a Roman **colonia**. The most outstanding example is the great German city of Cologne (known to Germans themselves as Köln), which started as **Colonia Claudia Agrippina**, named after the celebrated Agrippina who was wife of the Roman Emperor Claudius and mother of the notorious Nero. Similarly, the Roman town of **Lindum Colonia** has become the modern Lincoln.

In those parts of continental Europe where Roman power was dominant for centuries, Latin names have often survived into modern times with little change. Spanish Cadiz, for instance, is recognisably from the Latin **Gades**; French Marseilles is not much altered from Latin **Massilia**; the Roman town of **Londinium** became London; and **Mediolanum** is clearly the parent of modern Milan.

The Roman baths at Bath

Sometimes the connection between the Latin and the modern name is more obscure. For example, it was the Roman habit to call places which had medicinal waters by the name **Aquae**. ("Taking the waters" was as popular with the ancient Romans as it was with nineteenth-century Europeans.) The Roman city of Bath was known to them as **Aquae Sulis**. Cities in Gaul which bore the name **Aquae** sometimes show that origin today in the unlikely form "Aix", e.g. **Aquae Sextiae** became the modern Aix-en-Provence. Paris was originally called **Lutetia Parisiorum**, i.e. the Marshland of the Parisii. As often happened, the name of the tribe became the name of the town.

Perhaps the most surprising survival forms of Latin place-names are those assumed by towns named after Julius Caesar and Emperor Augustus, e.g.

Latin Form	Modern Form
Forum Iulii	Fréjus (French)
Augusta	Aosta (Italian)
Caesarea Augusta	Zaragoza (Spanish)

The status of **civitas** ("community") was given to many Roman settlements, e.g. **Civitas Turonum** ("the community of the Turones") and **Civitas Aurelianensis** (called after Aurelius). In the course of time, the word **civitas** disappeared, leaving only the name of the local tribe or the name of the founder. For example, the communities just mentioned became Turin and Orléans. In Spain, the word **civitas** survived in the form *ciudad* (derived from the accusative **civitatem** shorn of its ending **-em**), e.g. Ciudad Real and Cuidad Rodrigo. Interestingly, the final "d" of Ciudad is pronounced as a "t".

Most of the place-names incorporating Latin elements are survivals from ancient times. There are some in England, however, which are comparatively recent creations, e.g. Weston-super-Mare, Linstead Magna, Linstead Parva, Ampney Crucis, Ashby Puerorum (Ashby financially supported the boy choristers of Lincoln Cathedral), and Toller Fratrum (Toller contributed to the upkeep of the monastic brothers in Forde Abbey near by).

Other towns and villages are associated with bishops (**episcopi**), e.g. Huish Episcopi and Wick Episcopi; and some have been honoured with the patronage of royalty, e.g. Lyme Regis, Brompton Regis, Grafton Regis, etc. The best known of these royally-distinguished towns, Bognor Regis, received the title "Regis" as recently as 1929 after King George V had recuperated there following a serious illness.

Aenigma   **House word search**

Find seventeen words associated with Roman houses.

Words are in straight lines (horizontal, vertical or diagonal), but never backwards. The same letters may be used in more than one word. (*The solution is on page 142.*)

	a	b	c	d	e	f	g	h	i	j	k
1	D	V	E	S	T	I	B	U	L	U	M
2	C	U	B	I	C	U	L	U	M	U	T
3	U	A	I	A	N	U	A	U	I	T	R
4	L	N	N	R	U	M	N	L	M	A	I
5	I	D	S	E	S	I	Y	M	P	B	C
6	N	R	U	A	L	T	A	A	L	E	L
7	A	O	L	B	S	D	L	A	U	R	I
8	L	N	A	I	L	A	O	S	V	N	N
9	A	T	R	I	U	M	C	M	I	A	I
10	F	E	N	E	S	T	R	A	U	L	U
11	P	O	S	T	I	C	U	M	M	S	M

Unit X (Chapters 33–38)

Exercenda

1 *What are these dates?*

(a) Kalendis Novembribus
(b) Nonis Juliis
(c) Nonis Ianuariis
(d) Idibus Aprilibus
(e) Idibus Octobribus
(f) pridie Kalendas Februarias
(g) pridie Nonas Iunias
(h) ante diem vi Kalendas Decembres
(i) a.d.vii Idus Maias
(j) a.d.iv Nonas Septembres

2 *Write these dates in their Latin form:*

(a) Christmas Day (25 December)
(b) Boxing Day (26 December)
(c) Hogmanay (31 December)
(d) New Year's Day (1 January)
(e) Hallowe'en (31 October)
(f) St Valentine's Day (14 February)
(g) St Andrew's Day (30 November)
(h) St George's Day (23 April)
(i) St Patrick's Day (17 March)
(j) St David's Day (1 March)
(k) American Independence Day (4 July)
(l) Epiphany (6 January)

Chariot racing

3 *Translate:*

(a) Cornelia est tristissima, sed amica eius est etiam tristior quam ea.
(b) quis est crudelior illo tyranno superbo?
(c) Roma statim discessit et Neapolim quam celerrime rediit.
(d) Sextus versus Aeneidis pessime recitavit, Marcus optime.
(e) quod Romae diutius manere noluit, Brundisium brevissimo itinere petivit.
(f) tu puer es ignavissimus, Sexte. cur non diligentius laboras?
(g) vidistine umquam spectaculum mirabilius? aurigae equos ferocissime incitant.
(h) coquus Cornelii cenam optimam paraverat; convivae cibum meliorem numquam antea ederant.
(i) nemo est eruditior grammatico nostro; plura quam Eucleides scit.
(j) cuius nomen est praeclarius quam Caesaris?

4 *Pair off each deponent verb with the verb which has roughly the same meaning:*

.... (a) conabuntur   (i) dixisti

.... (b) egreditur   (ii) redibo

.... (c) locutus es   (iii) mansimus

.... (d) regrediar   (iv) exit

.... (e) ingrediebantur   (v) temptabunt

.... (f) morati sumus   (vi) discesserunt

.... (g) profecti sunt   (vii) intrabant

5 *Translate:*

(a) dum Eucleides loquitur, pueri e domo egredi subito constituerunt.

(b) Troia multos annos obsessa a Graecis deleta est.

(c) aestate tres menses Baiis morabantur.

(d) viatores prima luce profecti ad urbem quinque post horis pervenerunt. eos tribus diebus sequemur.

(e) servum, qui e fundo effugere conabatur, vilicus duabus horis consecutus est.

(f) discipulus a grammatico castigatus domum regressus est.

(g) "statim ad ludum proficiscimini, pueri! cur adhuc domi moramini?"

(h) Aeneas multa passus tandem ad Italiam venit.

6 *Flavia's reply to Cornelia's letter (Chapter 35)*

Flavia Corneliae SPD

cotidie tabellarios vehementer exspectabam sed, quamquam ad patrem epistolas complures ferebant, nihil mihi tulerunt. hodie tamen prid.Id. Nov. accepi tandem epistolam quam tu Non. Nov. scripsisti. maximam laetitiam cepi ex tua epistola atque
5 vehementer gaudeo et quod celerrime epistolae meae respondisti et quod epistola tua celerius solito allata est.

    hic in villa nostra sine metu vivimus. quid tamen dicam de urbe Roma in qua aedificia incenduntur et incolae insularum saepe flammis opprimuntur? praeterea, ut mihi videtur, cives Romani
10 domo nocte exire propter metum non audent convaluitne iam Eucleides, homo miserrimus, tam graviter a praedonibus vulneratus?

Atramentaria

Penna

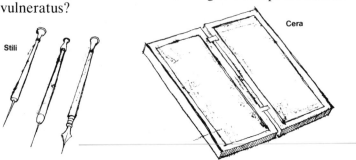

Stili

Cera

18

si Eucleidi est periculosissimum nocte foras ire, licetne tibi exire etiam interdiu?   si non licet, cur non Baias statim regrederis?   olim
15 mirabilis mihi videbatur urbs Roma et ibi habitare vehementissime volebam, nam valde cupiebam theatrum visitare, Amphitheatrum Flavium videre, vestimenta pretiosissima emere.   nunc tamen gaudeo quod mihi necesse est Baiis morari.

Valerium mox videbis, nam, ut dixisti, cras Brundisio
20 proficiscetur.   propter hoc tibi invideo.   Valerius enim est adulescens pulcherrimus et fortissimus.

scribe, sis, quam celerrime!   ama me et vale!

laetitia, -ae (f), joy, pleasure   foras ire, to go outside
solito, than usual   interdiu, during the daytime
praeterea, besides   pretiosus, -a, -um, expensive

cupio, -ere (3), cupivi, cupitum, to desire, long for
invideo, -ere (2), invidi, invisum (+ dat.), to envy

Note that **vehementer** has some slightly unusual meanings in this letter. It appears to be one of Flavia's favourite words.

7 *Translate:*

Arion and the Dolphin

temporibus antiquis in Graecia fuit citharoedus praeclarissimus, Arion nomine, qui Corinthi habitabat.   etiam Italia capta erat voce et arte eius.

olim Arion, famam et pecuniam petens, ad Siciliam et Italiam
5 navigavit.   ibi in magnis urbibus maximas divitias comparavit. parans igitur Corinthum Tarento regredi, navem Corinthiam et nautas Corinthios conduxit, nam Corinthiis modo credebat.   ita in hac nave divitias sua arte comparatas audacter imposuit, nihil timens. sed nautae Corinthii, paulum Tarento progressi, mox constituerunt
10 divitias Arionis rapere et ipsum necare.

tum clamavit Arion perterritus "omnes meas divitias vobis dabo si me vivere patiemini."   sed frustra eis persuadere conatus est.

tandem Arion "sine dubio" inquit "me necare in animo habetis. hoc unum tamen rogo.   patimini me cantare unum carmen!   deinde,
15 promitto, in mare desiliam."

cui Corinthii (nam valde volebant audire summum citharoedum cuius vocem nemo umquam postea auscultaret) "tibi licebit unum modo carmen cantare;   tum necesse erit finem et cantandi et vivendi facere."
20   itaque Arion, pulcherrimis vestibus indutus, cithara cantavit et in mare desiluit.   Arionem tamen servavit delphinus quidam, qui prope natabat dulcedine carminis captus.   eum enim per mare transportavit et in terram non procul a Corintho exposuit.   incolumis fuit et homo et vestis et cithara et vox.   inde Arion Corinthum
25 profectus est.   ad Periandrum regem Corinthiorum accessit et rem totam narravit.

rex, ubi illa navis Corinthia Corinthum advenit, nautas sine
tumultu ad se adduci iussit.   eos comiter allocutus est.   "de
Arione," inquit "qui iam sex menses in Sicilia et Italia moratur,
30 numquid scitis?"

"ita vero, o rex optime!" responderunt nautae.   "Arioni Tarenti
occurrimus.   ibi sine dubio adhuc moratur."

subito irrupit Arion, ita ut in nave indutus et citharam ferens.
tum nautae inopino visu attoniti, omnia confessi, a rege graviter
35 puniti sunt.

citharoedus, -i (*m*), singer who
   accompanied himself on the
   cithara
Corinthus, -i (*f*), Corinth
divitiae, -arum (*f.pl*), wealth,
   riches
Tarentum, -i (*n*), Tarentum
   (a port in Italy)
nauta, -ae (*m*), sailor
vivo, -ere (3), **vixi, victum,** to
   live
carmen, carminis (*n*), song
desilio, -ire (4), **desilui, desultum,**
   to jump down

postea, after that, afterwards
auscultaret, would hear
   (listen to)
dulcedo, dulcedinis (*f*),
   sweetness, charm
Periander, Periandri (*m*),
   Periander, ruler of Corinth
numquid scitis? Do you know
   anything at all?
inopino visu, by the unexpected
   sight
confiteor, -eri (2), **confessus sum,**
   to confess, admit

8 *Do not translate unless asked to do so, but answer in English the
questions which follow.*

Atalanta and Hippomenes

in Graecia habitabat puella quaedam, nomine Atalanta, quae non
modo pulcherrima erat sed celerius quam omnes viri currere
poterat.   olim de matrimonio oraculum consulebat.   cui respondit
deus "noli, o Atalanta, coniugem petere, nam coniunx fiet dominus
5 tuus neque tu tuo more vivere poteris."   hoc consilio dei sollicita
procos omnes vitabat; atque, quamquam multi eam in
matrimonium ducere volebant, duras matrimonii condiciones
Atalanta eis dabat.   omni enim proco "si celerius me curres,"
inquit "uxor tua ero.   si tamen a me victus eris, certe statim
10 necaberis."

quamquam hoc facere periculosum erat, multi viri currere
volebant.   itaque die constituta complures viri temerarii fortunam
temptabant.   eheu!   omnes victi sunt;   necati sunt omnes.

sed inter spectatores eo die sederat adulescens quidam, nomine
15 Hippomenes, qui Atalantam antea non viderat.   simul eam
spectavit, simul amavit.   morte ceterorum minime deterritus,
Atalantam coniugem petere constituit, neque amici eum retinere
poterant.   "certe illa celerrime currere potest, sed ego prior ad
finem cursus advenire possum.   Venus, quae amantibus favet,

20 auxilium mihi dabit." auxilium igitur a dea statim petivit; tria
mala aurea illa ei dedit.

postridie, ubi Hippomenes in arenam venit, ei superbe Atalanta
"nisi celerius quam ego curres," inquit "uxor tua fieri nolam."

cui respondit Hippomenes "quod te maxime amo, hoc periculum
25 temptare volo. tu si a me vinceris, uxor mea fies; ego si tu me
vinces, libenter moriar."

signa tubae dederant; adulescens ac puella summa celeritate iam
currebant. mox tamen, quamquam Hippomenes quam celerrime
currebat, puella facile antecessit. tum adulescens unum e tribus
30 malis ante puellam currentem coniecit. "hoc quidem" secum
cogitabat "puellam a cursu avertet." statim malum petit puella,
statim adulescens eam praetercurrit.

non diu tamen morata est puella; mox iterum praecedebat.
alterum igitur malum coniecit adulescens. iterum puella malum
35 petivit, iterum puellam consecutus est adulescens. sed Atalanta,
ubi clamores spectatorum audivit, multo celerius cucurrit.
Hippomenem praeteriit atque metae iam appropinquabat.
at Hippomenes "nunc, o dea," inquit "fer mihi auxilium!" tum
tertium malum longe coniecit. dum puella hoc malum petit,
40 Hippomenes ad finem cursus prior pervenit. victa est puella.
laetus ab arena puellam duxit victor.

matrimonium, -i (*n*), marriage
coniunx, coniugis (*m/f*),
   husband, wife
more tuo vivere, to live in your
   own way, maintain your
   independence
procus, -i (*m*), wooer, suitor

durus, -a, -um, harsh
die constituta, on the appointed
   day
prior, first
cursus, -us (*m*), race, track
faveo (2) (+ *dat.*), to favour
malum, -i (*n*), apple
tuba, -ae (f), trumpet

21

(i) Comprehension Questions:

(a) What were the harsh conditions which Atalanta imposed on those who wished to marry her?

(b) Translate **eo die** (line 14) and explain why this case was used.

(c) What reason did Hippomenes give for taking the risk?

(d) What happened soon after the start of the race?

(e) How did Hippomenes deal with this problem?

(f) In what way did Atalanta react to this?

(g) What was different about the way he used the third apple?

(h) What is the difference in meaning between **praetercurrit** (line 32) and **consecutus est** (line 35)?

(ii) Discussion Points:

(a) What sort of answer might Atalanta have expected when she went to consult the oracle?

(b) Do you agree with the oracle's statement **tuo more vivere non poteris** (line 5)? Would this statement apply equally to men and women?

(c) **prior ad finem cursus advenire possum** (line 18): produce evidence from the passage to show that Hippomenes was not really as confident as he pretended to be.

(d) Why do you think Hippomenes appealed to Venus rather than any other god or goddess?

(e) Why did the author use **prior** (lines 18 and 40) instead of **primus?**

(f) What effect is the author trying to produce through the words **omnes victi sunt; necati sunt omnes** (line 13)?

(g) **simul eam spectavit, simul amavit** (line 15): why do you think the author repeated **simul**?

(h) Produce more examples from the passage where the author repeats words. State what effect you think he is trying to produce.

(i) Can you think of a common four-word English expression (not a translation) which conveys the meaning of the words quoted in (g)?

Footnote: Those who wish a more detailed account of this story and one which raises some interesting human issues, should turn to a translation of Ovid *Metamorphoses* X.560 ff.

Statue of Venus dating
from the fifth century BC

Derivanda

1 (a) *The following Latin comparatives/superlatives have been taken straight into English. Give the meaning of each word as used in English and Latin:*

major   minor   plus   optimum   minimum   maximum

(b) *Give the meanings of the following English words which are derived from Latin comparatives/superlatives:*

optimist   pessimist   majority   minority
minimal   maximise   plural   ameliorate

2 *List the Latin words from which these English words are derived, and give the meanings of the Latin and the English words:*

English word	Derived from	Meaning of Latin word	Meaning of English word
veteran gravity consecutive percussion utility castigate regression sanguinary			

3 *Use your knowledge of Latin to work out the meanings of the Latin phrases in bold type, which are commonly used in English:*

(a) To preserve national security, the trial of the spy will be held **in camera.**

(b) He bored his friends by telling them the same stories **ad nauseam**.

(c) A desperate man will often do **in extremis** things that he would not normally do.

(d) The club decided to form an **ad hoc** committee to discuss the erection of a new pavilion.

(e) As he was not a logical thinker, his arguments contained many a **non sequitur**.

(f) "So, naturalists observe, a flea
Hath smaller fleas that on him prey;
And these have smaller fleas to bite 'em,
And so proceed **ad infinitum**."
(Jonathan Swift)

4 *Here are some Latin words you may have used in English without realising they are Latin words. Check their Latin meanings in the vocabulary at the end of the book and their English meanings in an English dictionary, and see if there is any difference in usage:*

alibi   sinister   versus   album   via   memento
terminus   consensus   arbiter   finis   pauper   area

5 At the end of *Ecce Romani* Book 2, you were given some information about compounds.

(a) The vowels in some simple verbs change when used in compounds, e.g.:

facio   but   reficio
factum   but   refectum
teneo   but   retineo

(b) The last consonant of some prefixes may change to the consonant which follows it, e.g.:

in + mitto   becomes   immitto
in + ruo   becomes   irruo
con + mitto   becomes   committo

This type of change is called *assimilation* (**ad** + **similis**), a word which is itself a good example of assimilation.

Break the following verbs down into simple prefix and simple verb:

Compound verb	Simple Prefix and Verb
effugere	ex + fugere
assumere	
inhibere	
retinere	
abripere	
irrumpere	
collaborare	
decidere	
immittere	
annuntiare	
colligere	
colloqui	
recipere	
adigere	
insidere	
attingere	
apportare	
accipere	
afficere	
arripere	

Memoranda

1 *Translate the following mottoes/sayings which contain comparative adjectives/adverbs:*

fortior qui se vincit.	(family motto)
vita cara, carior libertas	(family motto)
ad maiorem Dei gloriam	(Jesuit motto)
spero meliora.	(family motto)
video meliora proboque, deteriora sequor.	(Ovid)
timor mortis morte peior.	

carus, -a, -um, dear   **deteriora,** worse things
probo (1), to approve

2 In Chapter 35, you met the expression

quo celerius ... eo celerius ...
the faster ... the faster ...

In mottoes, this type of expression is handled in much the same way as **is qui** (see Unit IX), i.e. it can appear as **quo ... eo ...,** or as **eo ... quo ...,** or **eo** may simply be omitted. Similar balanced expressions occur with the following correlatives:

tam ... quam ...	as ... as ...
tot ... quot ...	as many ... as ...
tantus ... quantus ...	as great ... as ...
talis ... qualis ...	such ... as ...

Translate the following quotations which contain correlatives:

quo timoris minus est, eo minus periculi.	(Livy)
quo certior, eo tutior.	(Information Unit of RAF)
firmior quo paratior.	(family motto)
quid est tam incertum quam talorum iactus?	(Cicero)
quot homines, tot sententiae.	(Terence)
tam mihi mea vita quam tua tibi cara est.	(Cicero)
frumentum tanti fuit quanti iste aestimavit.	(Cicero)
talis est respublica qualis eius natura qui illam regit.	(Cicero)
tantam eorum multitudinem nostri interfecerunt quantum fuit diei spatium.	(Caesar)
tot mala sum passus quot in aethere sidera lucent.	(Ovid)

tutus, -a, -um, safe
talorum iactus, a throw of dice
sententia, -ae (*f*), opinion
tanti, of as great value
aestimo (1), to value

spatium, -i (*n*), space
malum, -i (*n*), evil, hardship
aether, -eris (*m*), heaven, sky
sidus, sideris (*n*), star

3 *The following mottoes/sayings contain deponent verbs:*

altiora sequimur.	(Family motto)
non progredi est regredi.	(an Urban District Council)
aut pugna aut morere.	(an R.A.F. Squadron)
non omnis moriar.	(Horace)
res ipsa loquitur.	(Cicero)
vir sapit qui pauca loquitur.	(anon.)
interdum stultus bene loquitur.	(proverb)

sapio (3), to be wise
interdum, sometimes

4 *Match the Latin sayings with their near-equivalent English proverbs/ sayings in the box below:*

amicus certus in re incerta cernitur.	(Ennius)
pares cum paribus congregantur.	(Cicero)
forsan miseros meliora sequentur.	(Virgil)
quem di diligunt adulescens moritur.	(Plautus)
canis timidus vehementius latrat quam mordet.	(Q. Curtius)
quo plures eo hilariores.	
carrus boves trahit.	
plus vident oculi quam oculus.	

cerno (3), to perceive, see   **diligo** (3), to love
par, paris, equal   **hilaris, -is, -e,** happy, merry
forsan, perhaps

> His bark is worse than his bite.
> Two heads are better than one.
> The more the merrier.
> Every cloud has a silver lining.
> A friend in need is a friend indeed.
> Birds of a feather flock together.
> Putting the cart before the horse.
> Only the good die young.

5 Catullus was a contemporary of Julius Caesar. He died in his thirties but left poetry of great intensity and directness, describing principally his love-hate relationship with his sweetheart Lesbia. Such was his love for Lesbia at the time when he wrote the following poem, that even a small event like the death of her pet sparrow moved him to call upon the deities of Love and Passion (Venus and Cupid) and "all men of finer feeling" **(quantum est hominum venustiorum)** to mourn Lesbia's sad loss.
    The metre here is the eleven-syllable line called the Hendecasyllabic.

Cupid

Lesbia's Sparrow

lugete, o Veneres Cupidinesque
et quantum est hominum venustiorum!
passer mortuus est meae puellae,
passer deliciae meae puellae,
5 quem plus illa oculis suis amabat;
nam mellitus erat suamque norat
ipsam tam bene quam puella matrem;
nec sese a gremio illius movebat,
sed circumsiliens modo huc modo illuc
10 ad solam dominam usque pipiabat.
qui nunc it per iter tenebricosum
illuc, unde negant redire quemquam.
at vobis male sit, malae tenebrae
Orci, quae omnia bella devoratis!
15 tam bellum mihi passerem abstulistis!
o factum male, o miselle passer,
tua nunc opera meae puellae
flendo turgiduli rubent ocelli.

lugeo (2), to mourn
venustus, charming, sensitive
passer, -eris (*m*), sparrow
deliciae, -arum (*f. pl*), darling, pet
mellitus, honey-sweet
suam norat, knew its mistress
nec = neque
sese = se
gremium, -i (*n*), lap, bosom
circumsiliens, hopping around
modo ... modo ..., now ... now ...
usque pipiabat, it chirped continually

tenebricosus, full of darkness, gloomy
negant quemquam, they say that no one
vobis male sit! a curse on you!
tenebrae Orci, darkness of the Underworld
bellus, beautiful, pretty
factum male, evil deed
tua opera, thanks to you
flendo, with weeping
rubeo (2), to be red

misellus, turgidulus and **ocellus** are diminutives of **miser, turgidus** (swollen) and **oculus.** (Cf. **parvulus** and **parvus.**)

6 The following poem contains several diminutives. It was addressed by the Emperor Hadrian (AD 76–138) to his soul when he was dying. The translation is by Lord Byron.

animula vagula blandula,
hospes comesque corporis,
quae nunc abibis in loca—
pallidula, rigida, nudula,
nec, ut soles, dabis iocos?

Ah! gentle, fleeting, wav'ring sprite,
Friend and associate of this clay!
*   To what unknown region borne,*
Wilt thou now wing thy distant flight?
No more with wonted humour gay,
*   But pallid, cheerless, and forlorn.*

animulus: diminutive of **animus**
blandulus: diminutive of **blandus**
vagulus: diminutive of **vagus**
pallidulus: diminutive of **pallidus**
nudulus: diminutive of **nudus**

The Emperor Hadrian

Miranda   THE CALENDAR

Over the centuries, people have devised various ways of measuring time. The most common has been a system, based on the movements of the sun and the moon, which concentrates on three main divisions of time — the day, the lunar month (**luna, -ae** (*f*), the moon) and the solar year (**sol, solis** (*m*), the sun).

The main problem in devising a calendar was reconciling these different times. The earth takes just under 24 hours to revolve on its axis; the time from one new moon to the next is roughly 29½ days so that twelve lunar months amount to only 354 days; the earth takes 365 days 5 hours 48 minutes 46 seconds to travel round the sun.

The Roman year originally had only ten months (304 days), beginning in March, which explains why September to December were the "seventh" to "tenth" months rather than the 9th to 12th as they are today. The second king of Rome added January and February, bringing the total number of days in the year to 355. It was left to the priests to add an extra month, whenever they wished, to bring the calendar into line with the solar year. By the first century BC, however, the priests were often subjected to political pressure, either to insert an extra month to allow someone to remain longer in power, or to delay the insertion to keep someone's period of office as short as possible.

When he became dictator, Julius Caesar decided to regularise the calendar so that every year was more or less the same length. His scientists calculated that the solar year lasted 365¼ days. In 46 BC, therefore, when he introduced what is now called the Julian Calendar, he decreed that that year should last 445 days to bring the calendar into line with the solar year (which shows how badly the calendar had become distorted) and that, in future, each year should last 365 days, with every fourth year having an extra day added to take account of the quarter day. Unfortunately, the priests to whom control of the calendar was entrusted misunderstood their instructions and added the extra day every third year.

In AD 4, the Emperor Augustus remedied this mistake by restoring the Julian calendar as it was intended to be; and, just as the name of the "fifth" month had been changed from Quintilis to Julius to honour Julius Caesar, so Augustus changed the name of the "sixth" month from Sextilis to Augustus to honour himself.

The Julian Year turned out to be 11 minutes 12 seconds longer than the solar year and over the centuries this began to mount up so that, by AD 1582, there was an error of ten days. Pope Gregory XIII therefore decreed yet another change — that there should be no leap year at the turn of a century unless that year could be divided exactly by 400. It is this Gregorian Calendar which we operate today.

The Emperor Augustus

The names of the months are all adjectives, agreeing with the noun **mensis, -is** (*m*), month (understood), or with one of the special days (**Kalendae, Nonae, Idus**):

Ianuarius:	the "doorway" to the year (**ianua**)
Februarius:	the month of purification (**februare,** to purify)
Martius:	the month dedicated to Mars, the God of War
Aprilis:	the month when the earth opens up (**aperire**)
Maius:	called after Maia, the mother of Mercury (See also footnote.)
Iunius:	*may* be connected with the goddess Juno
Iulius:	dedicated to Julius Caesar (previously called **Quintilis,** the "fifth" month)
Augustus:	dedicated to Augustus (previously called **Sextilis,** the "sixth" month)
September:	the "seventh" month
October:	the "eighth" month
November:	the "ninth" month
December:	the "tenth" month

Footnote: Others see a connection with the Latin word **maior**, viz. after plants "open" in April, they become "bigger" in May.

Aenigma   Find the words and score the points

	1	2	3	4	5	6	7	8	9	10	11	12	13	14	15	16	17	18	19
1	P	E	S	T	O	L	A	U	D	A	T	R	I	U	M	Q	U	A	M
2	S	E	Q	U	E	R	E	M	A	G	I	S	T	E	R	R	E	O	S
3	L	U	P	O	S	S	E	Q	U	I	D	E	M	I	S	I	T	U	S
4	V	I	S	U	M	E	B	A	M	A	G	N	O	P	E	R	E	S	I

State the row and column in which the word starts. All words appear horizontally, and the same letters may be used as often as you wish.

  How to score: Add together the number of the row in which the word appears, the number of the column where the word starts, and the number of letters in the word, e.g.

Clue: "I am"   Answer: **sum**

Score: 4 (row 4) + 3 (column 3) + 3 (3 letters in **sum**) = 10 points

N.B. Some words may be found in more than one place. Those marked ** appear twice; those marked *** appear three times.

Total possible points amount to over 1000. (*Solution on page 142*)

1 I was taking
2 she sent
3 greatly
4 I go
5 what?
6 praise!
7 you (*sing.*) are going ***
8 he gives
9 down from
10 to follow
11 you (*sing.*) buy
12 through
13 by a thing ***
14 big (*abl.sing.masc.*)
15 to be able
16 I terrify
17 take!
18 things (*nom.*)
19 follow!
20 themselves **
21 you (*sing.*) drive

22 and
23 of a horse
24 if **
25 (to) there
26 I stand
27 indeed
28 but
29 the same (*masc.*)
30 more
31 ever
32 a bone
33 you (*sing.*) are **
34 I bought
35 she praises
36 wolves (*acc.*)
37 he is
38 seen (*acc.*)
39 teacher
40 all right!
41 frighten!
42 by whom (*fem.*)

43 you (*nom.sing.*)
44 me
45 them
46 I sent
47 girl's dress
48 you (*sing.*) wish
49 placed (*nom.*)
50 you (*acc. sing.*)
51 give!
52 by force
53 he ***
54 who (*masc.*)
55 love!
56 main room
57 that (thing)
58 by a wolf
59 force (*nom.*)
60 three (*gen.*)
61 a thing (*acc.*)
62 than
63 foot

30

Unit XI (Chapters 39–44)

Exercenda

1 *Translate:*

(a) nuntius ad Caesarem in Britanniam transgredi parantem venit.

(b) cives matri liberos servare conanti auxilium tulerunt.

(c) custodes furem vestimenta surripientem prehenderunt.

(d) Augusto principe, Romani multos populos superaverunt.

(e) servi vestimenta civium in balneis se exercentium custodiebant.

(f) incolae, qui ruina aedificii sepulti erant, clamores adiuvantium audire non poterant.

(g) Cicerone consule, Catilina consilium scelestum in populum Romanum cepit.

(h) mihi multa roganti nihil ille respondit.

(i) homines miserrimi lapidibus ex plaustro cadentibus oppressi sunt.

in (+ *acc.*), against

2 *Translate:*

(a) Cornelius rogavit quando Titus ad Thermas profectus esset.

(b) nonne sciebas quid nuntius dixisset?

(c) vidistine quid faceremus?

(d) cum ianuam aperuisset, in villam ingressa est.

(e) nondum cognoverant unde viator venisset.

(f) cum scirent quo in periculo essemus, auxilium ferre constituerunt.

(g) audivistisne quo servi ivissent cum a fundo effugissent?

(h) cum sororem meam alloquebar, subito sensi cur domi manere voluisset.

(i) nesciebamus cur praedones Eucleidem vulneravissent.

(j) cum cognovissent quales homines essetis, vos adiuvare nolebant.

3 *These sentences may both be translated in the same way:*

cum coquus vocatus esset, convivae cenam laudaverunt.
coquo vocato, convivae cenam laudaverunt.

In the following sentences, change the **cum** *clauses to Ablative Absolutes, and Ablative Absolutes to* **cum** *clauses:*

(a) cum barbari superati essent, Romani gaudebant.

(b) fratre ad ludum profecto, Cornelia sola domi manebat.

(c) cum vestimenta surrepta essent, custodes furem petiverunt.

(d) pecunia data, Tito licebat in balneas ingredi.

(e) omnibus rebus paratis, viatores profecti sunt.

(f) cum velamen inventum esset, Pyramus gladio stricto se occidit.

4 *Translate:*

(a) leo visus Thisben magnopere terruit.

(b) leone viso, Thisbe in speluncam fugit.

(c) leonem visum valde timuit Thisbe.

(d) vestimentis exutis, Titus et amici eius in balneas intraverunt.

(e) epistolam a Cornelio scriptam ad urbem nuntius ferebat.

(f) epistola a Cornelio scripta, nuntius ad urbem profectus est.

(g) nuntius ad urbem profectus Romam tribus diebus advenit.

(h) nuntius ad urbem profectus Romam tribus diebus adveniet.

(i) servo dormiente, vestimenta a fure surrepta sunt.

(j) tabellarius epistolam senatori ad Curiam profecturo tradidit.

5 *Translate:*

Bravery rewarded

iam diu urbs Roma a Porsinna, rege Etruscorum, obsidebatur atque
cives multa et gravia propter cibi inopiam patiebantur.   itaque
C. Mucius, adulescens nobilis, audax consilium cepit.   solus enim
in hostium castra penetrare constituit;   sed timens ne, si patrum
5 iniussu iret, forte a custodibus Romanis prehensus retraheretur ut
transfuga, senatum adiit.

  "transire Tiberim" inquit, "patres, et intrare, si possim, castra
hostium volo.   ibi, si di adiuvant, Porsinnam necare in animo
habeo."
10   senatores eum interrogabant quomodo hoc facere posset sed,
consilio audito, eum laudatum dimiserunt.

  gladio intra vestem celato, Mucius statim profectus est.   cum
Tiberim transiisset, castra hostium clam ingressus in magna turba
prope regis tribunal stetit.   duos tamen viros ibi sedentes conspexit,
15 similibus vestimentis indutos.   timens rogare uter Porsinna esset,
illum occidit qui nobilior esse videbatur.   scriba tamen regis, non
rex ipse, ita occisus est.   statim a custodibus prehensus ante regis
tribunal tractus est Mucius.

  tum regi interroganti quis esset et cur scribam necavisset Mucius
20 respondit. "Romanus sum" inquit "civis.   C. Mucium vocant.

hostis hostem occidere volui.   quamquam ego te necare non potui,
longus post me est ordo iuvenum idem petentium.   non omnes te
occidere conantes vitabis."

    rex igitur, simul ira commotus periculoque perterritus, ignes
25 afferri iussit, nam in animo habebat Mucium cruciatu interrogare
quae consilia iuvenes cepissent.

    sed Mucius "ecce!" inquit.   "nunc sentire potes quam vile corpus sit
eis qui magnam gloriam vident," dextramque in ignem iniecit neque
abstraxit.

30   prope attonitus miraculo virtutis rex, cum de tribunali desiluisset,
iuvenem ab ignibus amoveri iussit.   "tu vero abi!" inquit.   "in te
magis quam in me hostilia ausus es.   propter tuam virtutem te
liberatum ad tuos cives remitto."   Mucium legati a Porsinna
Romam secuti sunt pacem petentes.   postea cives propter dextram
35 paene deletam Scaevolam cognomen ei dederunt.

Adapted from Livy, II.12

inopia, -ae (f), scarcity	**vilis, -is, -e**, cheap, worthless
castra, -orum (n.pl), camp	**dextra, -ae** (f), right hand
timens ne, fearing that	**miraculum, -i** (n), marvel
patrum iniussu, without the permission of the senators	**virtus, -utis** (f), bravery
	in te, against yourself
transfuga, -ae (m), deserter	**hostilia audere,** to commit the daring act of an enemy
tribunal, -alis (n), platform	
uter, utra, utrum, which (of two)	**legatus, -i** (m), ambassador
	Scaevola, -ae (m), "the left-handed"
scriba, -ae (m), clerk	
ordo, ordinis (m), line, row	**cognomen, -inis** (n), surname, nickname
ignis, -is (m), fire	
cruciatu, under torture	

6 *Do not translate unless asked to do so, but answer in English the questions which follow:*

Horatius Cocles

Tarquinius rex a Romanis expulsus, cum a Porsinna auxilium
petiisset, multis cum militibus in agros Romanorum mox rediit,
urbem Romam obsessurus.   milites eius, cum collem vicinum,
nomine Ianiculum, subito impetu cepissent, inde ad flumen celeriter
5 decurrebant.   tum cives perterriti, armis relictis, ad urbem
confugiebant, muris se defensuri.   Pons tamen Sublicius iter paene
hostibus dedit.   unus vir, Horatius Cocles, in statione pontis illo die
forte positus, urbem servavit.

    Horatius enim, ceteris omnibus iam refugientibus, in aditu pontis
10 stetit talia clamans: "si praesidium relinquetis, cives, frustra
fugietis.   nisi pontem defendetis, mox in Capitolio erunt plures
hostes quam nunc in Ianiculo.   vos pontem interrumpite!   ego ipse
hostibus resistam."

    quibus dictis, Horatius in aditum pontis progressus ipso miraculo

15 audaciae obstupefecit hostes.   manebant enim cum Horatio duo
    modo comites, Spurius Larcius ac Titus Herminius, ambo viri
    praeclarissimi.   una cum his impetum hostium paulisper sustinuit.
        interea cives pontem interrumpebant; subito magna voce
    clamaverunt "statim redite, viri!   pons paene interruptus est!" tum
20 Horatius, minima parte pontis iam relicta, comites recedere
    iussit.   comitibus regressis, ipse hostibus resistebat solus.   hostes,
    clamore sublato, undique in unum hostem tela coniecerunt;
    virumque vulneratum iam detrudebant, cum simul fragor interrupti
    pontis, simul clamor Romanorum paulisper impetum sustinuit.
25   tum Horatius graviter vulneratus "Tiberine pater," clamavit "haec
    arma et hunc militem accipe!"   deinde armatus in Tiberim desiluit
    et, multis superincidentibus telis, incolumis ad alteram ripam
    tranavit.

impetus, -us (*m*), attack	**obstupefacio** (3), **-feci, -factum,**
flumen, fluminis (*n*), river	to stupefy, astound
in statione pontis, on guard on	**sustineo** (2), **-ui, -tentum,** to
the bridge	check, hold back
aditus, -us (*m*), approach	**telum, -i** (*n*), weapon
praesidium, -i (*n*), defence,	**detrudo** (3), **-trusi, -trusum,** to
fortification	push aside, dislodge

(i) Comprehension Questions:

(a) List in chronological order the events described in lines 1–10.
(b) Translate the participle **obsessurus** (line 3). Why was this tense used?
     Quote from the passage another example of this usage.
(c) List two examples of an Ablative Absolute in which a perfect participle
     is used, and two where a present participle is used. Explain why these
     tenses were used.
(d) Why did the author use **vos** and **ego** in line 12?
(e) Why do you think the author put **solus** (line 21) at the end of the
     sentence?
(f) To what does Horatius refer when he says **haec arma et hunc militem**
     (line 25)?

(ii) Discussion Points:

(a) What effect is the author trying to produce by using **simul** twice (lines
     23, 24)?
(b) What difference would it make to the meaning of the sentence if the
     words **illo die forte** (line 7) were placed between **urbem** and **servavit**?
(c) Explain the religious significance of Horatius saying **"Tiberine pater"**
     (line 25).
(d) Do you think this incident happened before or after the story about
     Scaevola? Give your reasons.

Note: A dramatic and exciting treatment of this story is to be found in
Lord Macaulay's *Lays of Ancient Rome.*

Derivanda

1 List the Latin verbs from which these English words are derived, and give the meanings of the Latin and the English words. Consult your dictionary if necessary.

English word	Latin Verb	Meaning of Latin verb	Meaning of English word
convalescence subsequent repellent surreptitious recognition sentiment valedictory collapse			

2 Complete the blanks to form English words derived from Latin:

studium, -i (*n*) : stud _   stud _ _ _   stud _ _ _ _
annus, -i (*m*)   : ann _ _ _   ann _ _ _ y   ann _ _ _ _ _ _ _ y
sequor, -i (3)   : sequ _ _   sequ _ _ _ e sequ _ _ _ _ _ l
credo, -ere (3)   : cred _ _   cred _ _ _ r cred _ _ _ e
mare, maris (*n*) : mar _ _ _   mar _ _ a   mar _ _ _ r
fumus, -i (*m*)   : fum _ s   fum _ _ _ _ e p _ _ fum _
migro (1)   : migr _ _ e migr _ _ t   emigr _ _ _ _ _

3 In Unit III, you learned that -able/-ible words mean "able to be -ed". What do the following mean?

    navigable   incredible   acceptable   irresistible
    edible   invincible   visible   preferable
    laudable   culpable   retractable   defensible

Sometimes, this type of word means "able to do something". Use your knowledge of Latin to work out the meanings of the following:

    terrible   sensible   responsible   stable   possible

4 (a) Give the meanings of the following English words and then suggest what you think is the basic meaning of the ending "-fy":

    fortify   notify   stultify   ossify   rectify

   (b) The force of the ending "-fy" has changed slightly in the following. Consider their meanings with the help of a dictionary.

    pacify   verify   mortify   signify   identify

35

5 *The ending "-tor" means "the person who does something." Work out the meanings of the following Latin words:*

emptor	navigator	victor	pastor
creator	captor	monitor	rector

All of these, except the first, have been taken straight into English. Try to explain any differences in the meanings of the words as used in English and in Latin.

6 (a) *Many English words ending in -ant/-ent are identical to the stem of the Latin present participle, e.g.:*

"student" comes from studens, **student**is
"agent" comes from agens, **agent**is

Give the nominative and genitive singular of the present participles from which the following come, and show how the meaning of the Latin participle relates to the English word:

detergent	migrant	inhabitant	current	incumbent
patient	regent	continent	servant	constituent
eloquent	accident	resurgent	occupant	respondent

(b) *Also related to the Latin present participle are many English nouns ending in -ance/-ence or -ancy/-ency, e.g.:*

"ambulance" comes from **ambulans, ambulantis**
"agency" comes from **agens, agentis**

Give the nominative and genitive singular of the present participles from which the following come, and show how the meaning of the Latin participle relates to the English word:

sequence	audience	eloquence	consequence
ignorance	stance	expectancy	currency
regency	science	constituency	preference

Memoranda 1 *Translate the following sayings/mottoes which use present participles:*

audentes fortuna iuvat.	(Virgil)
timeo Danaos et dona ferentes.	(Virgil)
perseveranti dabitur.	(family motto)
vox clamantis in deserto	(Vulgate)
sero venientibus ossa	(proverb)
amantium irae amoris integratio est.	(Terence)
locum tenens	
deo volente	

iuvo (1), to help
Danai, -orum (*m.pl*), Greeks
et, even

ossa, bones, scraps (i.e. the remains of a meal)
integratio, -onis (*f*), renewal

2 *Match the Latin sayings with their near-equivalent English proverbs/ sayings in the box below:*

flamma fumo est proxima.	(Plautus)
dum spiro, spero.	(family motto)
venienti occurrite morbo!	(Persius)
mutato nomine, de te fabula narratur.	(Horace)
dimidium facti qui coepit habet.	(Horace)
noli equi dentes inspicere donati!	(Terence)
lupus in fabula.	(Plautus)
rem acu tetigisti.	(Terence)

spiro (1), to breathe
morbus, -i (*m*), sickness, illness
dimidium, -i (*n*), half
coepit, (he) has begun
acus, -us (*f*), needle, pin-point

Don't look a gift-horse in the mouth.
Meet trouble half way!
Talk of the devil.
You've hit the nail on the head.
Where there's life there's hope.
There but for the grace of God go I.
There is no smoke without fire.
Well begun is half done.

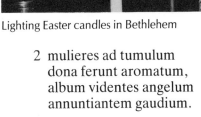

Lighting Easter candles in Bethlehem

3 *An Easter Carol*

(Tune **"Deus tuorum militum"**, No. 42 in The Church Hymnary, 3rd Edition)

1 surrexit Christus hodie
  humano pro solamine
  mortem qui passus corpore
  miserrimo pro homine.

2 mulieres ad tumulum
  dona ferunt aromatum,
  album videntes angelum
  annuntiantem gaudium.

3 mulieres o tremulae,
  in Galilaeam pergite!
  discipulis hoc dicite
  quod surrexit Rex gloriae!

pro solamine, for the salvation
passus, supply **est**
tumulus, -i (*m*), hill
dona aromatum, gifts of spices

albus, -a, -um, white
tremulus, -a, -um, trembling
pergite! hasten!
quod, that

4 *In this poem, Martial compares his friend's little dog, Issa, to Lesbia's sparrow. The metre is Hendecasyllabic.*

A Pet Dog

Issa est passere nequior Catulli;
Issa est purior osculo columbae;
Issa est blandior omnibus puellis;
Issa est carior Indicis lapillis;
Issa est deliciae catella Publi.
hanc tu, si queritur, loqui putabis;
sentit tristitiamque gaudiumque.

Martial, *Epigrams* I.109

nequior, naughtier
osculum, -i (*n*), kiss
columba, -ae (*f*), dove
blandus, -a, -um, charming, gentle
Indicus, -a, -um, Indian

lapillus, -i (*m*), gem, pearl
catella, -ae (*f*), puppy
queror (3), to whimper, whine
tristitia, -ae (*f*), sadness
-que . . . -que . . ., both . . . and . . .

Miranda   1 MORE ABOUT THE CALENDAR

Although the Kalends of March were supplanted by the Kalends of January as the first day of the year, the former continued to be an important day for married women because on that day they generally received presents from their husbands. It was also a special day for female slaves since, on 1st March, they were feasted by the mistress of the household.

The Kalends were an important day in every month for those who had borrowed money, as interest payments were due on that day. The account-book, in which these payments were recorded, was called a **calendarium**, and it was from this Latin word that the English word "calendar" was derived.

The English word "date" originates from the habit of writing at the head of a letter or document the words **littera data** or **epistola data** ("the letter was given") followed by the figures of the day and month.

One of the derivatives of the Latin word **sextus** is the word "siesta". The Roman day (from sunrise to sunset) was divided into twelve equal hours and the sixth hour began at midday.

By a strange coincidence, the English word "noon" is a derivative of the Latin adjective **nonus**, "ninth". This adjective was originally applied to one of the services of the Church because it began at 3p.m. (the ninth hour). At a later date, this service was moved to midday and the word "noon" came to be associated with "midday" as well as with the service.

2 THE SIGNS OF THE ZODIAC

The sky seems to form a sphere around the earth. Round this celestial sphere there are twelve constellations which form a kind of belt along which the sun appears to traverse the sky in the course of a year. This "belt" is called the Zodiac.

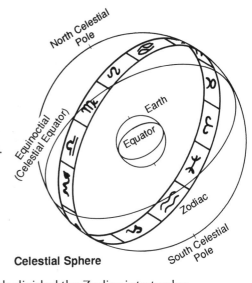

Celestial Sphere

Astrologers from ancient times onwards divided the Zodiac into twelve equal parts. To each of these parts was given the name of a constellation which was visible in that area of the sky. The Zodiacal Circle (to give it its full name) means the circle of living creatures, because all the signs, except Libra (the Balance), relate to animate beings.

AQUARIUS

PISCES

ARIES

TAURUS

CAPRICORNUS

GEMINI

CANCER

Aquarius:	The Water-carrier	(21 January–19 February)
Pisces:	The Fishes	(20 February–20 March)
Aries:	The Ram	(21 March–20 April)
Taurus:	The Bull	(21 April–20 May)
Gemini:	The Twins	(21 May–21 June)
Cancer:	The Crab	(22 June–23 July)
Leo:	The Lion	(24 July–23 August)
Virgo:	The Maiden	(24 August–23 September)
Libra:	The Balance	(24 September–22 October)
Scorpio:	The Scorpion	(23 October–22 November)
Sagittarius:	The Archer	(23 November–22 December)
Capricornus:	The Goat	(23 December–20 January)

SAGITTARIUS

SCORPIO

LIBRA

VIRGO

LEO

Astrology, which claims to be able to describe the character and life-possibilities of each individual by scrutiny of the exact date and hour of birth, is often described dismissively as a "pseudo-science"; but it still has its defenders, and there is no doubt that the horoscopes which figure largely in newspapers and magazines still command a large following.

Aenigma Visit to the Baths

On this visit, Titus has spent all morning at the Baths and has used most of the facilities, some of them more than once. Trace the order of his activities. Only vertical and horizontal moves are allowed. (*The solution is on page 143.*)

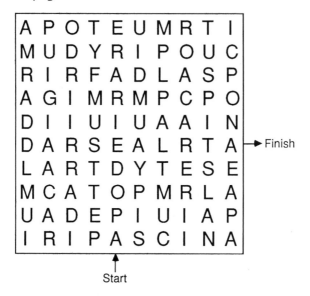

```
A P O T E U M R T I
M U D Y R I P O U C
R I R F A D L A S P
A G I M R M P C P O
D I I U I U A A I N
D A R S E A L R T A  → Finish
L A R T D Y T E S E
M C A T O P M R L A
U A D E P I U I A P
I R I P A S C I N A
```

↑
Start

Plan of the Stabian Baths at Pompeii.

Note that the women did not have a frigidarium. The hypocaust served both sections.

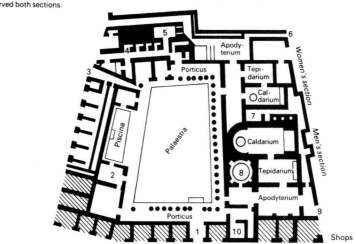

Key: 1 Men's entrance
      2 Shallow pool
      3 Side entrance
      4 Separate baths
      5 Latrine
      6 Women's entrance
      7 Hypocaust
      8 Frigidarium
      9 Side entrance
      10 Waiting room (for slaves)

0   10   20m

Unit XII (Chapters 45–49)

Exercenda

1 *Translate, paying particular attention to the tenses:*

   (a) sentimus clamores a custodibus non audiri.

   (b) sensimus clamores a custodibus non audiri.

   (c) sentimus clamores a custodibus non auditos esse.

   (d) sensimus clamores a custodibus non auditos esse.

   (e) speramus vos Romam mox redituros esse.

   (f) speravimus vos Romam mox redituros esse.

   (g) scivistine complura hostium oppida a militibus nostris capta esse?

   (h) responderunt se Brundisium iter facere in animo habere.

   (i) constabat Romanos multo fortius quam hostes pugnavisse.

   (j) pro certo habebam multos gladiatorum eo die morituros esse.

2 *Translate:*

   (a) viatores rogavimus qui essent, unde profecti essent, cur eo venissent, quo irent.

   (b) vidimus hostes urbem intrare.

   (c) vidimus hostes urbem intrantes.

   (d) vidimus ubi hostes urbem intrarent.

   (e) conspexistine magnam turbam servorum qui in viis clamabant?

   (f) audivimus magnam turbam servorum in viis clamantium.

   (g) audivimus magnam turbam servorum in viis clamare.

   (h) in urbe nobis ostenderunt multa et mira.

   (i) nobis ostenderunt ubi multa et mira in urbe videre possemus.

   (j) nobis ostenderunt multa et mira nos in urbe videre posse.

3 *Study this example:*

   iam intrat Caesar.
   quid clamavit Titus?

   Titus clamavit Caesarem iam intrare.

   Following the above pattern, complete the following groups of sentences and then translate them:

   (a) Cornelius semper est negotiosus.
       quid dicis?

       dico _____

   (b) viae sunt plenae civium.
       quid vides?

       video _____

(c) gladiatores cuncti contra pulvinar constiterant.
quid dixisti?

dixi _____

(d) leo saevissimus captivos necabit.
quid putaverunt spectatores?

spectatores putaverunt _____

(e) Androcles omnium consensu liberatus est.
quid audivistis?

audivimus _____

(f) Aurelia gladiatores videre non cupit.
quid sentiebat Cornelius?

Cornelius sentiebat _____

(g) princeps a gladiatoribus salutatur.
quid videbas?

videbam _____

(h) Caesar amphitheatrum mox aperiet.
quid intellexerunt cives?

cives intellexerunt _____

(i) Romani templum Iudaeorum deleverant.
quid sciebat Cornelius?

Cornelius sciebat _____

(j) Marcus brevi tempore togam virilem sumet.
quid respondit pater?

pater respondit _____

4 *Translate:*

A Fable: The Wolf and the Lamb

haec fabula a Phaedro, poeta Romano, narrata est.
    olim lupus et agnus, siti compulsi, ad eundem rivum venisse
dicuntur.   superiore ripae parte stabat lupus, inferiore agnus.
    lupus autem, cum in rixam inire vellet, agnum rogavit cur aquam
5 turbulentam sibi bibenti faceret.   agnus, quamquam lupum
magnopere timebat, negavit se scire quomodo id fieri posset.
ostendit enim aquam a lupo ad se, non a se ad lupum decurrere.
    quo audito, lupus adhuc rixans dixit agnum sex ante mensibus sibi
maledixisse.   cui tamen respondit agnus se duos modo menses
10 natum esse; se igitur haec facere non potuisse.
    tum lupus, iam ira valde commotus, exclamavit patrem agni certe
sibi maledixisse, atque haud diutius moratus agnum correptum
devoravit.
    quid haec fabula vult dicere?   Phaedrus ipse dixit hanc fabulam
15 scriptam esse quod vellet illos homines castigare qui fictis causis
innocentes opprimerent.

agnus, -i (*m*), lamb	**maledico** (3) (+ *dat.*), to speak
sitis, -is (*f*), thirst	ill (of), abuse, curse
turbulentus, -a, -um, muddy	**fictus, -a, -um**, false, made up
	causa, -ae (*f*), reason,
	accusation

5 *Do not translate unless asked to do so, but answer in English the
questions which follow the poem by Phaedrus.*

The Wolf and the Lamb

Aesop's Fables were written in Greek. The poet Phaedrus (first century
AD) retold them in Latin verse. Here is the original poem on which
Exercenda Exercise 4 was based. The metre is iambic trimeter.

ad rivum eundem lupus et agnus venerant,
siti compulsi.   superior stabat lupus,
longeque inferior agnus.   tunc fauce improba
latro incitatus iurgii causam intulit.
5 "cur" inquit "turbulentam fecisti mihi
aquam bibenti?" laniger contra timens:
"qui possum, quaeso, facere, quod quereris, lupe?
a te decurrit ad meos haustus liquor."
repulsus ille veritatis viribus
10 "ante hos sex menses male" ait "dixisti mihi."
respondit agnus: "equidem natus non eram."
"pater hercle tuus ibi" inquit "maledixit mihi."
atque ita correptum lacerat iniusta nece.
haec propter illos scripta est homines fabula,
15 qui fictis causis innocentes opprimunt.

tunc, then	**queror, queri** (3), **questus sum,** to complain
fauce improba incitatus, urged on by monstrous appetite	**haustus, -us** (*m*), drinking-place
iurgium, -i (*n*), quarrel	**veritas, -atis** (*f*), truth
laniger, -era, -erum, wool-bearing	**equidem,** I (very emphatic)
contra, in reply	**lacero** (1), to tear to pieces
qui, how	**iniustus, -a, -um,** unjust
quaeso, please tell me	**nex, necis** (*f*), violent death

To answer some of the following questions a comparison will have to be made between the above poem and the prose version in Exercenda 4.

(i) Comprehension Questions:

(a) The wolf used three different pretexts for killing the lamb. What were they? How did the lamb prove the first two wrong?

(b) Quote the Latin phrase Phaedrus uses for "pretexts".

(c) The Latin verb **nocere** means to "harm". Using your knowledge of Latin prefixes, give the literal meaning of **innocens** (poem, line 15). The adjective **improbus** (poem, line 3) means "wicked". What would **probus** mean?
What would be the Latin opposite of **iniustus** (poem, line 13).

(d) Translate the words **repulsus veritatis viribus** (poem, line 9).

(ii) Discussion Points:

(a) Phaedrus uses another word for each of the words **lupus, agnus** and **aqua**. What are these words, and what are the more colourful ideas they conjure up?

(b) Contrast the effects produced by line 7 of the poem and line 6 of the prose passage. What does Phaedrus achieve by the broken pattern of the words?

(c) Which of the expressions **agnum correptum devoravit** (prose, line 12) and **correptum lacerat iniusta nece** (poem, line 13) do you think is more effective? Give reasons for your answer.

(d) What do the words **improba** (line 3), **latro** (line 4) and **iniusta** (line 13) tell us about the poet's attitude towards the wolf?

(e) The poem quotes the direct speech used by the animals, whereas the prose version reports what they said indirectly (reported speech). Which technique do you prefer? Give reasons for your answer.

Derivanda

1 *Here are other English words derived from Latin present participles. (Cf. page 36.) List the Latin participles (Nominative and Genitive singular) and give the meanings of the participles and of the English words:*

English word	Latin Participle	Meaning of Participle	Meaning of English word
adjacent incipient clamant latent apparent intelligent repugnant cogent consistent recumbent errant			

2 *The following words are derived from Latin supines. List the Latin supines, present infinitives and meanings, and give the meanings of the English words:*

English word	Latin Supine	Present Infinitive and meaning	Meaning of English word
conversion expression recognition obsession passion repetition admission contradiction percussion perdition inception friction			

3 **bene,** *"well" and* **male,** *"badly" are frequently used as prefixes. Use your knowledge of Latin to find the meanings of the following English words:*

benediction	malediction
benevolent	malevolent
benefactor	malefactor
benefaction	malefaction
beneficent	maleficent
beneficence	maleficence
benefit	—
beneficial	—
beneficiary	—

4 *Latin word families*

Use your knowledge of some of the following words to deduce the meanings of those you have not yet met:

Noun	Adjective	Adverb	Verb
terror	terribilis terrificus	terribiliter	terrere
onus	onerosus onustus onerarius	onerose	onerare
pulchritudo	pulcher	pulchre	—
lacrima	lacrimosus lacrimans lacrimabilis	lacrimose	lacrimare
attentio	attentus	attente	attendere
taciturnitas	tacitus taciturnus	tacite	tacere
turba	turbidus turbulentus	turbide turbulente	turbare
diligentia	diligens	diligenter	diligere
prudentia providentia	prudens	prudenter	providere

5 *Use your knowledge of Latin to work out the meanings of these Latin expressions used in English:*

(a) My parents were delighted when at the end of the horse-jumping competition I was acclaimed **victor ludorum**.

(b) In taking action without the prior approval of his committee the chairman was acting **ultra vires**.

(c) The phrase **fidei defensor** appears on British coins in the abbreviated form F.D.

(d) The accused Thomas Black, **alias** Terence Brown, will appear in court tomorrow.

(e) The **impetus** for the project was lost when the chairman resigned.

(f) Explain to me the **pros** and **cons** of your plan.

(g) My brother was given the degree of **Doctor Litterarum** by his **alma mater**.

Memoranda

The Athenian philosopher Socrates, who was born about 470 BC and was put to death in 399 BC

1 *The following famous sayings involve the use of an Accusative and Infinitive clause:*

homo sum: humani nil a me alienum puto. (Terence)
I am a man: I consider that everything concerning man concerns me. (Literally, "nothing human is alien to me".)

omnem crede diem tibi diluxisse supremum. (Horace)
Believe that every day which has dawned is your last.

Socrates putabat se esse civem totius mundi. (Cicero)
Socrates believed that he was a citizen of the whole world.

dilucescere (3), **diluxisse,** to dawn   **mundus, -i** (*m*), the world
supremus, -a, -um, last

2 *Three Epigrams of Martial*

(a) scribere me quereris, Velox, epigrammata longa;
     ipse nihil scribis, tu breviora facis.
Martial I.110

(b) difficilis facilis, iucundus acerbus es idem:
     nec tecum possum vivere, nec sine te.
Martial XII.47

(c) nubere vis Prisco; non miror, Paula; sapisti:
     ducere te non vult Priscus; et ille sapit.
Martial IX.5

queror (3), to complain   **acerbus, -a, -um,** bitter
iucundus, -a, -um, pleasant

3 *Student Song*

(The music may be found at No. 1 in the *Scottish Student's Song Book.*)

1 Gaudeamus igitur
  Iuvenes dum sumus.
  Post iucundam iuventutem
  Post molestam senectutem
  Nos habebit humus.

2 Ubi sunt qui ante nos
  In mundo fuere?
  Vadite ad superos,
  Transite ad inferos
  Ubi iam fuere.

3 Vita nostra brevis est;
  Brevi finietur.
  Venit mors velociter,
  Rapit nos atrociter.
  Nemini parcetur.

4 Gaudeamus igitur
  Iuvenes dum sumus.
  Post iucundam iuventutem
  Post molestam senectutem
  Nos habebit humus.

gaudeamus, let us rejoice   **inferi, -orum** (*m.pl*), the gods below
humus, -i (*f*), the earth   **finio** (4), to finish
fuere = fuerunt   **velociter,** swiftly
vado (3), to go   **parco** (3) (+*dat.*), to spare

4 *Latin literature is full of sayings which are often quoted and well worth remembering:*

poeta nascitur, non fit.	(proverb)
dulce est desipere in loco.	(Horace)
facilis descensus Averno.	(Virgil)
vox audita perit, littera scripta manet.	(quoted by Wm. Caxton)
multi famam, conscientiam pauci verentur.	(Pliny)
mea mihi conscientia pluris est quam omnium sermo.	(Cicero)
parturiunt montes, nascetur ridiculus mus.	(Horace)
o quid solutis est beatius curis?	(Catullus)
eheu fugaces, Postume, Postume, labuntur anni.	(Horace)

nascor (3), to be born	**pluris,** more valuable
desipio (3), to play the fool	**sermo, -onis** (*m*), talk
in loco, on occasion, occasionally	**parturio** (4), to give birth, be in labour
Avernus, -i (*m*), the Underworld*	**curas solvere,** to remove cares, relax tensions
fama, -ae (*f*), gossip, rumour	**fugax, -acis,** fleeting
vereor (2), to fear	**labor** (3), to slip away

Note: The Romans regarded Lake Avernus as the entrance to the Underworld.

Miranda   CONSULTING THE ORACLE

When the ancient Romans and Greeks wished to obtain guidance on some difficult decision affecting national life (e.g. whether or not to go to war), they would consult an oracle (**oraculum,** which is from the same root as the verb **orare,** "to beg" or "to pray"). Oracles were usually to be found in temples dedicated to one of the great gods, especially Apollo or Jupiter.

Questions were put to a priestess while she was in a trance. Her answers tended to come out as a stream of meaningless gibberish which was then interpreted by the priests for the enquirer. This sounds like an invitation to fraud and deception, but these oracles must have given sound advice on the whole because they were consulted for many centuries. If prophecies of future events had turned out to be false, the credibility of the oracle would soon have been destroyed.

The priests occasionally issued the oracular response in obscure, sometimes ambiguous language. For example, according to the Roman poet Ennius, when Pyrrhus (King of Epirus in northern Greece) asked if he should attack the Romans, the oracle at Delphi replied:

aio te, Aeacida, Romanos vincere posse.

aio, I declare   **Aeacida,** O son of Aeacus (i.e. Pyrrhus)

Aegeus, king of Athens, consulting a prophetess. From an Athenian vase, about 400 BC.

What two meanings can this line have? Which meaning did Pyrrhus take out of it? Which turned out to be true?

When the sons of Tarquinius Superbus, the last king of Rome, were on a mission to the oracle at Delphi, they decided to ask which of them would succeed their father. They were given the response:

imperium summum Romae habebis qui vestrum, o iuvenes, osculum matri tulerit.

"Young men, the one of you who first kisses his mother will hold supreme power in Rome."

Both of them took the response literally, but their cousin Brutus ("the dull one") interpreted it differently. When he stepped ashore from the ship which brought them back from Greece, he pretended to stumble and kissed the earth of Italy as he fell. When Tarquin was expelled, Brutus was one of the two consuls whom the Romans elected to rule them in place of the one king.

Yet another example of ambiguous advice led to the overthrow of Croesus, King of Lydia and ruler of a vast empire. When he was at the height of his power, he sent messengers to the oracles in Delphi and Thebes to ask if he should invade Persia. The replies he received were the same: "If Croesus attacks the Persians, he will destroy a mighty empire."

When Xerxes, the King of Persia, invaded Greece and seemed about to capture Athens, the Delphic oracle advised the Athenians that "the wooden wall" would keep them and their children safe. Some interpreted this to mean that they should retreat into the citadel which was surrounded by a wooden palisade. Themistocles, however, claimed that the wooden wall referred to ships and persuaded the Athenians to build up their fleet. Although still greatly outnumbered when the navies ultimately met, the Athenians defeated the Persians and thus saved both Athens and Greece.

Aenigma   Chariots and Gladiators

Find nineteen words associated with the amphitheatre and the circus.
The words are in straight lines (horizontal, vertical or diagonal) but never
backwards. The same letters may be used in more than one word.

The solution is on page 143.

	a	b	c	d	e	f	g	h	i	j
1	A	P	P	A	R	I	T	O	R	V
2	T	A	R	F	O	L	U	D	I	N
3	E	N	M	E	T	A	E	N	Q	A
4	S	E	L	R	T	N	A	V	H	U
5	S	M	I	R	M	I	L	L	O	M
6	E	H	O	O	D	S	A	F	C	A
7	R	M	M	I	T	T	E	R	B	C
8	A	A	R	E	N	A	U	R	I	H
9	B	E	S	T	I	A	R	I	I	I
10	M	P	U	L	V	I	N	A	R	A

1 They fought with net and trident.
2 The emperor's seat.
3 Gate-keeper.
4 Sea-fight.
5 Ticket.
6 The mid-day fighters.
7 _ _ _ _ _ **et circenses.**
8 "Let him go!"
9 _ _ _ _ **circenses.**
10 _ _ _ _ **ac deliciae.**
11, 12 _ _ _ , **vinciri,** _ _ _ _ **que necari.**

13 _ _ _ **habet!**
14 The "fish man".
15 The area for fighting.
16 Androcles' opponent.
17 Wild beast fighters.
18 The trainer.
19 The ends of the **spina.**

Wild beast
fighters

Unit XIII (Chapters 50–54)

Exercenda

1 *Translate:*

   (a) pueri in atrium celeriter cucurrerunt ut sororem terrerent.

   (b) pueri in atrium tam celeriter cucurrerunt ut sororem terrerent.

   (c) captivus Troianos magno studio obsecrabat ut sibi parcerent.

   (d) captivus Troianos tanto studio obsecrabat ut ei parcerent.

   (e) multi homines in urbem venerunt ut captivos spectarent.

   (f) tot homines in urbem venerunt ut captivos spectare non omnes possent.

   (g) consules, ut orator saepe monuerat, impetum in hostes fecerunt.

   (h) consules orator saepe monuerat ut impetum in hostes facerent.

   (i) diligenter laborabat ut omnes se laudarent.

   (j) tam diligenter laborabat ut omnes eum laudarent.

2 *Translate:*

   (a) patri persuadebimus ut nos ad amphitheatrum ducat.

   (b) patri persuadebimus nos ad amphitheatrum ire velle.

   (c) nos multa rogavit.

   (d) nos rogavit ut Romam rediremus.

   (e) nos rogavit cur Romam rediremus.

   (f) cives monui urbem maximo in periculo esse.

   (g) cives monui ut consuli parerent.

   (h) consul senatores tandem arcessivit ut eis diceret quot milites Romani Cannis necati essent.

3 *Translate:*

Ulysses and the Lotus Eaters

Ulixes, postquam Graeci Troiam captam deleverunt, cum comitibus suis ad Ithacam domum redibat.   Ithacae iam appropinquabant cum, magna tempestate coorta, a cursu acti sunt.   novem dies maximis ventis acti multa et gravia passi sunt.

5   decimo tamen die, labore defessi nauseaque affecti, ad insulam quandam pervenerunt, ubi habitabant ei qui a Graecis Lotophagi appellabantur; lotum enim florem edebant.   si quis lotum edit, omnia oblitus, in illa insula morari neque umquam inde abire vult.   nam ibi modo illud medicamentum somniferum inveniri

10 potest.

    Ulixes autem tres nautas in Lotophagos misit.   eos iussit ab incolis salutatis cibum aquamque comiter petere.   statim profecti amice accepti sunt a Lotophagis qui eis lotum edendam dederunt. itaque obliti cur eo missi essent, ibi manere volebant.

15   Ulixes, cum sensisset illos nautas iam multas horas abesse, primo
      iratus, deinde sollicitus fuit.   constituit tandem cognoscere cur
      comites non rediissent.   itaque haud moratus cum ceteris comitibus
      in Lotophagos profectus est.   cum nautas semisomnos sub
      arboribus iacentes conspexisset, statim sensit lotum eis datam esse.
20   quamquam eos iterum iterumque iussit ad navem regredi, illi se
      movere nolebant.
          primo dixit se eos sub arboribus iacentes relicturum esse; deinde
      ira commotus imperavit ut tres nautas vincirent.   hoc modo illos
      tres nautas invitos ad litus traxerunt atque sine mora adhuc vinctos
25   in navem tulerunt.   tum Ulixes comites iussit navem statim solvere.
      sciebat enim ceteros comites, si lotum edissent, domum non
      regressuros esse.   itaque sine aqua, sine cibo ab illa insula
      discesserunt, multa alia in itinere passuri.

cursus, -us (*m*), course
nausea, -ae (*f*), sickness
lotus, -i (*f*), lotus
si quis, if anyone
obliviscor, -i (3), **oblitus sum**, to
  forget
medicamentum, -i (*n*), drug

somniferus, -a, -um, sleep-
  bringing
nauta, -ae (*m*), sailor
edendus, -a, -um, to be eaten, to
  eat
vincio (4), **vinxi, vinctum**, to
  bind, tie up
navem solvere, to set sail

4 *Do not translate unless asked to, but answer in English the questions
   which follow:*

The Sibylline Books

de libris Sibyllinis haec memoria tradita est.
    anus quaedam incognita olim ad Tarquinium Superbum regem
adiit novem libros ferens.   dicebat eos esse divina oracula atque
regem hortata est ut eos emeret.   Tarquinius anum rogavit

5   quantum pecuniae vellet.   mulier immensum pretium poposcit.
quo audito, rex ridens exclamavit anum certe insanam esse.
     tum illa, tribus libris in ignem prope positum iniectis, regem
interrogavit num reliquos sex eodem pretio emere vellet.   sed
Tarquinius multo magis risit dixitque anum iam sine dubio delirare.
10 quibus dictis, mulier statim tres alios libros in ignem iniecit
atque regem placide rogavit ut tres reliquos eodem illo pretio
emeret.
     quo viso, Tarquinius iam serius atque attentior intellexit se
oportere eam constantiam non neglegere.   itaque libros tres
15 reliquos emit nihilo minore pretio quam quod erat petitum pro
omnibus.   constat eam mulierem statim digressam postea nusquam
visam esse.   omnes autem credebant eam certe esse sibyllam.   illi
igitur tres libri in templo positi "Sibyllini" appellati sunt.   ad eos
quasi ad oraculum quindecimviri adeunt, cum di immortales publice
20 consulendi sunt.

Aulus Gellius I.19

memoria, -ae (*f*), tradition, account	**constantia, -ae** (*f*), persistence, determination
anus, -us (*f*), old woman	**nihilo minore pretio**, for no lower a price
incognitus, -a, -um, unknown (to him)	**sibylla, -ae** (*f*), prophetess
num, whether, if	**quindecimviri**, the fifteen priests (See page 69.)
reliquus, -a, -um, remaining	**cum consulendi sunt**, whenever (they) have to be consulted
deliro (1), to be mad	

(i) Comprehension Questions:

(a) What claim did the old woman make about the books, and what did she ask the king to do?

(b) To what does the word **eos** (line 3) refer?

(c) What was the king's reaction when he heard the price?

(d) What did the old woman do in response to the king's reaction?

(e) How often did this happen?

(f) What price did the king eventually pay?

(g) What was the attitude of the old woman throughout the incident?

(h) Why were they called the Sibylline Books?

(i) Where did the old woman come from at the start of the story and where did she go to at the end?

(ii) Discussion Points:

(a) What changes took place in the attitude of the king at each stage? Do you think his initial reaction and these changes were justified?

(b) Suggest examples of situations in which the priests might be asked to consult the Sibylline Books.

(c) Explain the difference between **ad oraculum** and **quasi ad oraculum** (line 19).

Derivanda

1 Complete the blanks to form English words derived from Latin:

sol, solis (*m*)   sol _ _ ,   sol _ _ _ _ m,   sol _ _ _ ce,   p _ _ _ sol

avis, avis (*f*)   av _ _ _ y,   av _ _ _ _ r,   av _ _ _ _ _ _

mos, moris (*m*)   mor _ _ ,   mor _ _ _ _ y,   mor _ _ e,   immor _ _

hilaris, -is, -e   hilar _ _ _ ,   hilar _ _ _ _ ,   e _ hilar _ _ _ _ n

oro (1)   or _ _ _ r,   or _ _ _ _ n,   a _ or _

levis, -is, -e   lev _ _ y,   lev _ _ _ _ _ _ n,   a _ lev _ _ _ e

orno (1)   orn _ _ _ _ t,   orn _ _ _ _ _ _ l,   _ _ orn,   orn _ _ e

2 In Units IX and X you met the Latin noun endings **-tas** and **-tudo**, corresponding to the English endings "-ty" and "-tude". Complete the following columns and give the meanings of the English words:

Latin adjective	Latin noun	English noun	English meaning
levis gravis hilaris utilis facilis humanus nobilis vicinus fidelis timidus urbanus virilis immortalis	levitas	levity	
rectus magnus multus latus longus altus solus fortis	rectitudo	rectitude	

3 The ending **-sor** has the same meaning as the ending **-tor** which you met in Units VI and XI. The **-tor** nouns come from Latin verbs whose supine ends in **-tum**, the **-sor** nouns from verbs whose supine ends in **-sum**. Although in Latin these words mean "the person who", in English they can also mean "the thing which". Here is a list of English nouns ending in **-tor/-sor**. Give the supine, present infinitive and meaning of the Latin verbs from which they are derived and also the meanings of the English nouns:

English noun	Latin Supine	Present Infin. and meaning	Meaning of English noun
oppressor visor cursor actor creditor depositor compositor tractor extractor injector interrogator inventor interlocutor			

4 *Use your knowledge of Latin to explain the meanings of the words in bold print:*

(a) I am glad to find you **convalescent** after such a serious illness.

(b) After the fire, the youth appeared in court on a charge of **arson.**

(c) The **intrepid** members of the Red Arrows gave a dazzling display of skydiving.

(d) The shortest day of the year occurs at the winter **solstice.**

(e) Take your time! There is no great **urgency** to complete the work.

(f) Only **posterity** can decide whether or not the Prime Minister acted wisely in this affair.

(g) The young officer, showing remarkable **ingenuity**, accomplished all the tests set for him.

(h) Since we know your difficulties, we have tried to **alleviate** the heavy burden you have had to bear.

5 *Many Latin words have been taken straight into English. The following were used in daily newspapers over a period of only a few days. Check their Latin meanings in the vocabulary at the end of the book and their English meanings in an English dictionary, and see if there is any difference in usage:*

vacuum	cadaver	curriculum	forum
humus	medium	solarium	herbarium
aura	media	consul	aquarium

Memoranda INSCRIPTIONS

One of the most striking proofs of the extent to which the Romans penetrated the whole known world of antiquity is the abundance of inscriptions which have survived in Europe, Africa and Asia. Even in an area as distant from Rome as Britain, well over 2000 inscriptions have been found. These not only tell us a great deal about the distribution of Roman forts, camps and walls and about the troops who manned them, but also bring us face to face with the actual words which, for example, a soldier used in dedicating an altar to Mithras or Jupiter, or a wife used in mourning the death of a husband, or a centurion the loss of a dear child.

At first sight, some of these inscribed stones appear undecipherable, a mere string of letters and parts of words; but, in many types of inscriptions, standard abbreviations occur and the various components of the inscription follow one another in a more or less regular sequence. It is this predictability which enables epigraphists (scholars who specialise in the study of inscriptions) to read defaced or mutilated monuments with reasonable certainty.

The following is the funerary (**funus, funeris** (*n*), burial) inscription of a **duplicarius** (a soldier on double pay as a reward for distinguished service) from the Roman town of Colchester. Opposite the inscription, the Latin text is given in full, together with an explanation of each word or phrase. There is an English translation below.

LONGINVS SDAPEZE	**LONGINUS SDAPEZE**
	praenomen / nomen
MATYCIFDVPLICARIVS	**MATYCI Filius DUPLICARIUS**
	father's name / rank
ALAPRIMA • TRACVMPAGO	**ALA PRIMA TRACUM PAGO**
	regiment / place of
SARDI • ANNO • XL • AEROR•XV	**SARDIco ANNOrum XL AERORum XV**
	origin / age / length of service
HEREDESEXSTESTAM F C	**HEREDES EX(s) TESTAMento Faciendum Curaverunt**
	those who erected the stone, and why
H. S. E	**Hic Situs Est**
	Where buried

English translation:

Longinus Sdapeze, son of Matycus, duplicarius of the first cavalry regiment of Thracians, from the Sardican district (modern Sofia), aged 40, of 15 years service, lies buried here. His heirs arranged for this monument to be put up in accordance with his will.

Note: In the second last line, **EXS** may be a variant spelling of **EX**, or it may stand for **EX SUO**.

At a later period, after about AD 50, funerary inscriptions followed a slightly different pattern. Instead of ending with **H.S.E.,** they began with **D.M. (Dis Manibus),** meaning either "to the spirits of the departed" or "to the Gods of the Underworld." Sometimes **D.M.S.** occurs (**Dis Manibus Sacrum**) — "Dedicated to the Gods of the Underworld." The following inscription comes from the Roman fort at Caerleon in South Wales.

Inscription	*Full Latin Text*
D • M •	**Dis Manibus**
G • VALERIVS • G • F	**Gaius VALERIUS Gai Filius**
GALERIA • VICTOR	**GALERIA VICTOR**
LVGDVNI • SIG • LEG II AVG	**LUGDUNI SIGnifer LEGionis II AUGustae**
STIP XVII • ANNOR XLV • CV	**STIPendiorum XVII ANNORum XLV**
RA • AGENT ANNIO PERPETVO H	**CURAm AGENTe ANNIO PERPETUO Herede**

English translation:

To the Gods of the Underworld: Gaius Valerius, son of Gaius, voting tribe Galeria, Victor, from Lugdunum (modern Lyons), standard-bearer of the Second Legion called Augustan, of seventeen years' service, 45 years old: Annius Perpetuus, his heir, set it up.

Tombstone of
Longinus Sdapeze

Other examples of Inscriptions

The following inscriptions are drawn from a wide range of sources. Write out the full Latin texts and translate them into English. Note that the lower case letters are not in the actual inscriptions but have been inserted to help you understand the full message. The solutions are on page 143.

1 From Ardoch in Perthshire
**DIS ● MANIBUS
AMMONIUS DAMIONIS f
COHortis I HISPANORUM
STIPENDIORUM
XXVII HEREDES
F ● C ●**

2 From York
**L ● DUCCIUS ● L ● F
VOLtinia tribu ● RUFINUS
VIENna ● SIGN ● LEG VIII
AN ● XXIIX
H ● S ● E**

Voltinia tribu, after the father's name often comes the voting tribe, "from the Voltinian tribe"

Vienna refers to Vienne in France.

Tombstone of
Lucius Duccius Rufinus

3 From Caerleon in Wales
**D ● M ●
T ● FLAVIUS CANDIDUS
ULP ● TRAIANA** (from Ulpia Traiana)
**M ● LEG II AUG ●
STI ● VII ● AN ● XXVII
FRAter ● Curavit**

4 From Carnuntum, Pannonia (Danube Province)

SEXT • TREBONIUS • Q • f
FABia tribu • PROCULUS
BERYto • CORNICULARius
LEG XV APOLlinaris
STIP XIII • AN XXX
H • S • E

cornicularius, chief clerk
Berytus, Beirut

5 From Tipasa in Mauretania
   The tombstone of Calliste, erected by her mother, Panathenais

D • M • S •
CALLISTE VIXIT ANNIS XVI
MES III HOR VI ET S̸
NUPTURA IDIBUS OCT
MORITUR IIII IDUS OCT.
PANATHENAIS MATER PIA
KARae FILiae FECIT

MES = mensibus
HOR = horis
S̸ = semisse, half

6 From Siscia in Pannonia
   The tombstone of Leburna, manager of a troupe of mime-actors

D • M •
POSITUS EST HIC
LEBURNA MAGISTER MIMARIORUM
QUI VIXIT ANNOS PLUS MINUS CENTUM
ALIQUOTIES MORTUUS SUM
SED SIC NUMQUAM

aliquoties, several times
In line 4, there is a change from the 3rd
to the 1st person. The reference is to his
performances on the stage.

Faced with the ambiguity of oracles and the problem of getting to the remote spots where they operated, the Romans turned to other systems of divination to find out if the omens were favourable before they decided to embark on any enterprise either in groups or as individuals. There were many types of happenings which were thought to disclose the favour or opposition of the gods to a particular course of action. To interpret these, the services of an **augur** (variously called a **haruspex** or an **auspex**) were essential.

The **haruspex** declared his augury after inspecting the entrails of animals which had been sacrificed to one of the gods. (**haru** + **spex** means literally "intestines-inspector".) He based his findings particularly on peculiarities in the appearance of the liver!

The **auspex** (derivation: **avis** + **spex**) was a "bird-watcher". He marked off an area of the sky (a **templum**) for scrutiny and drew his conclusions from the types and numbers of birds which appeared in his **templum** and from the direction of their flight. Since various birds were associated with particular gods (e.g. the eagle with Jupiter), there was a kind of rough logic in regarding them as messengers of the gods.

The brothers Romulus and Remus had recourse to augury to determine which of them should give his name to the new city they were preparing to set up. The historian Livy (Book I.6–7) describes the scene as follows:

"As they were twins and could not be distinguished by seniority, Romulus took as his **templum** the Palatine Hill, and Remus the Aventine, so that the gods, under whose sway these places came, should indicate by augury which brother should give his name to the new city and then rule over it once it had been established.

"It is said that an augury came to Remus first, in the form of six vultures; but no sooner had that omen been reported than twice as many birds appeared to Romulus.

"Both brothers were immediately proclaimed king by their own supporters, one group stressing priority, the other the number of birds. The argument which followed eventually led to bloodshed and Remus was killed."

From the very earliest period of their history, then, the Romans regarded augury as an essential part of both private and state religious observances; and, though faith in the efficacy of such practices faded in

the later Republic, even sceptics such as Cicero and Caesar were proud to hold religious office, Cicero as augur and Caesar as Pontifex Maximus, the official in charge of all state religion.

The more credulous of the Romans paid great attention to augury, which gradually extended its scope to include all manner of portents. There were five sorts of happenings that augurs regarded as significant:

(a) natural phenomena like thunder, lightning, eclipses, comets and earthquakes;
(b) the chirping or flight of birds;
(c) sightings of four-footed animals in unusual places;
(d) the behaviour of sacred chickens, whose eagerness or indifference in eating the food thrown to them was regarded as lucky and unlucky respectively;
(e) any odd occurrences (said to be **dira**), ranging from unusual and inexplicable sights and visions right down to mundane things such as stumbling, sneezing or spilling salt on a table or wine on clothes.

Even today, some of these superstitions command support!

Shakespeare, taking his cue from Plutarch's *Life of Caesar*, gives an impressive array of portents which appeared before the assassination of Julius Caesar:

CICERO: Why, saw you anything more wonderful?
CASCA: A common slave — you know him well by sight —
           Held up his left hand, which did flame and burn
           Like twenty torches joined; and yet his hand,
           Not sensible of fire, remained unscorched.
           Besides — I have not since put up my sword —
           Against the Capitol I met a lion
           Who glazed upon me and went surly by
           Without annoying me; and there were drawn
           Upon a heap a hundred ghastly women,
           Transformed with their fear, who swore they saw
           Men all in fire walk up and down the streets.
           And yesterday the bird of night did sit,
           Even at noon-day, upon the market-place
           Hooting and shrieking. When these prodigies
           Do so conjointly meet, let not men say
           "These are their reasons; they are natural."
           For I believe they are portentous things . . . .

Julius Caesar, Act I, Scene 3

Aenigma   Wedding Maze

Trace the three main stages of a Roman wedding. People, articles, events appear in chronological order. The numbers after the sub-headings show how many of these there are in each section. Arrows indicate starting and stopping points. Only vertical and horizontal moves are allowed. *(The solution is on page 143.)*

SPONSALIA (6)

```
A P O S P A
R S D R E T
E E P S O S
N T O U S C
E D N L L U
O A N U U M
```

NUPTIAE (7)

```
E M M A A T T U
U M A L F C E N
X E U T U G R I
P P S I I A A C
R T R B U G O G
O X A U S E I A
N E D T I C A F
U B A E R I L E
```

DEDUCTIO (6)

```
A C E V E S
T E A D E P
V R A R A E
A S C M T R
N E N I M E
U C A L I N
```

Unit XIV (Chapters 55–56)

Exercenda

1 *Translate:*

    (a) tempus est ad urbem regrediendi.

    (b) fur in templum intravit ad statuam deae surripiendam.

    (c) hostibus fortiter resistendo urbem servabimus.

    (d) nulla spes erat ex oppido eo die effugiendi.

    (e) boves in agros sunt reducendi.

    (f) quis dixit epistolas ad urbem esse referendas?

    (g) diligenter audiendo multa et utilia disces.

    (h) raeda e fossa equis extrahenda fuit.

    (i) quod cupidus sum tui videndi, Romam mox redibo.

    (j) gladiatores parati sunt et ad pugnandum et ad moriendum.

2 *Translate:*

    (a) tibi celeriter currendum est ut servum effugientem consequaris.

    (b) ad flumen transeundum rates militibus faciendae erant.

    (c) pueri, quod soli in vias urbis exierant, mihi reprehendendi erant.

    (d) civibus ad moenia concurrendum erat ut hostium impetum repellerent.

    (e) Aeneas et comites eius, parati ad multa patienda, Troia tandem profecti sunt.

    (f) cum servi eum necare conati essent, dominus mortem vitavit simulando se mortuum esse.

    (g) consules urbis defendendae causa magnum exercitum paraverunt.

    (h) servo roganti quid agendum esset dominus respondit cenam optimam parandam esse.

    (i) facultas matris adiuvandae omnibus liberis semper petenda est.

    (j) aquilifer aquilam in hostes ferendo ostendere volebat mortem non metuendam esse.

3 *Translate:*

(a) vestimenta servo sunt custodienda.

(b) consul, hostibus iam appropinquantibus, legatos ad pacem petendam misit.

(c) hic adulescens nuper uxoris petendae causa domo discessit.

(d) legati ad hostium ducem de captivis redimendis mittendi sunt.

(e) ignavo milite puniendo dux ostendere volebat sibi parendum esse.

(f) legio decima in finibus Treverorum hiemandi causa consedit.

(g) ad navigandum in Britanniam naves longae sunt reficiendae.

(h) alii ex militibus ad castra munienda manebant, alii ad agros vastandos exierunt.

(i) praedones nobis nullam effugiendi facultatem dederunt.

(j) Caesar vexillo proponendo signoque tuba dando nuntiavit nostros in hostes esse mittendos.

vasto (1), to lay waste

4 The Stag at the Spring

(1) *Translate:*

cervus olim, cum dies iam calidus esset, ad fontem quendam bibendi causa venit.   subito, imagine in aqua conspecta, bibere destitit.   cornua admiratus "o quam pulchra" inquit "cornua mea videntur!   quam similia arbori ramosae!"

5   deinde, cruribus in aqua conspectis, "o quam tenuia" inquit "crura mea videntur!   quam baculis similia!   haud mihi placent."
     at subito, vocibus venantium latrantibusque canibus perterritus, per campum summa celeritate fugere coepit, atque canes facile effugiebat.   cum tamen in silvas ingressus esset, ramis arborum
10 cornua impedita sunt.   quo facto, celeriter consecuti canes eum ferociter lacerare coeperunt.
     tum vero cervus moriens haec verba edidisse dicitur: "o me miserum!   quam stultus fui!   nunc demum intellego crura mea saepe vituperata me servare potuisse;   cornua maxime laudata me
15 perdidisse."
     quid ex hac fabula discere nos oportet?   ea quae rebus in secundis magni aestimantur, saepe in rebus adversis non usui sunt;   quae despiciuntur, ea saepe utilia sunt et laudanda.

cervus, -i (*m*), stag	**campus, -i** (*m*), open ground
calidus, -a, -um, warm	**edo** (3), **edidi, editum,** to utter
fons, fontis (*m*), fountain,	**demum,** at last
spring, pond	**vitupero** (1), to criticise, disparage
desisto (3), **destiti,** to stop,	**res secundae,** prosperous times
cease	**magni aestimare,** to value highly
cornu, -us (*n*), horn	**usui esse,** to be useful
crus, cruris (*n*), leg	**despicio** (3), **-spexi, -spectum,** to
venor (1), to hunt	despise

(2) *Do not translate unless asked to, but answer in English the questions which relate to both the poem and the prose passage. The metre is iambic trimeter.*

ad fontem cervus, cum bibisset, restitit
et in liquore vidit effigiem suam.
ibi, dum ramosa mirans laudat cornua
crurumque nimiam tenuitatem vituperat,
5 venantum subito vocibus perterritus
per campum fugere coepit, et cursu levi
canes elusit. silva tum excepit ferum,
in qua, retentis impeditus cornibus,
lacerari coepit morsibus saevis canum:
10 tunc moriens vocem hanc edidisse dicitur:
"o me infelicem! qui nunc demum intellego,
utilia mihi quam fuerint, quae despexeram,
et quae laudaram, quantum luctus habuerint."

Phaedrus

resto (1), **restiti,** to stop, stand still	**eludo** (3), **elusi, elusum,** to elude
effigies, -ei (*f*), reflection	**ferus, -i** (*m*), wild beast
nimius, -a, -um, excessive	**morsus, -us** (*m*), bite
venantum = venantium	**laudaram = laudaveram**
cursus, -us (*m*), running	**luctus, -us** (*m*), grief, distress
levis, -is, -e, light, effortless	

(i) Comprehension Questions:

(a) Explain the different meanings of the word **vox** as used in lines 5 and 10 of the poem.

(b) The phrase **ad fontem** appears in line 1 of both the verse and prose versions of the story but with different meanings for **ad**. What are these meanings?

(c) Translate the phrase **retentis impeditus cornibus** (poem, line 8).

(d) Translate the last three lines of the poem.

(ii) Discussion Points:

(a) The function of adjectives is to describe a noun in more detail. How do the following adjectives, as used in the poem, improve the picture?

      ramosa (line 3)   **nimiam** (line 4)   **levi** (line 6)

(b) Phaedrus chooses to say **morsibus saevis canum** (line 9) rather than simply **saevis canibus**. Why do you think he does this? Does it add anything to the picture?

(c) The prose passage and the poem use different constructions depending on **intellego** (prose line 13; verse line 11). Explain these constructions.

(d) Do you agree with what is said in the last paragraph of the prose passage? Can you produce other examples which support or contradict this view?

(e) Prose writers usually provide more factual information than poets, who tend to rely on the reader's imagination to fill gaps in a story. Quote three examples of this difference from these two versions of the fable.

(f) Discuss the different effect produced by the words **in aqua** (prose, line 2) and **in liquore** (poem, line 2).

(g) Discuss the irony of the words **silva excepit ferum** (poem, line 7).

Derivanda

1 *Some forms of the Latin Gerund/Gerundive are found in English words and phrases. Find their meanings in English and show their Latin root meaning. Use a dictionary if necessary.*

(a) Phrases used in their Latin form:

modus vivendi   onus probandi
modus operandi   locus standi
quod erat demonstrandum (QED)   mutatis mutandis
quod erat faciendum (QEF)

(b) Noun-forms used in English to denote something that "has to be done" have mostly retained their Latin forms:

Singular	*Plural*
addendum	addenda
corrigendum	corrigenda
memorandum	memoranda *
referendum	referenda *

*Note that memorandum and referendum are often pluralised as "memorandums" and "referendums" as if they were initially English words.

This anglicising process has been carried even further with the word **agenda**. Although plural in Latin, agenda is now treated as singular in English, and the plural is regularly written as "agendas".

(c) Anglicised forms:

dividend   tremendous
reverend   stupendous
legend   horrendous
graduand

(d) Feminine form used as a girl's name:

Amanda   Miranda

66

2 *Neuter forms of Latin Perfect Participles are frequently found in English. What do the following mean?*

Singular	Plural
datum	data
erratum	errata
stratum	strata
desideratum	desiderata
(obiter) dictum	(obiter) dicta
post scriptum	post scripta
(contracted to P.S.)	

3 *List the Latin words from which these English words are derived and give the meanings of the Latin words and of the English words:*

English word	Latin word	Meaning of Latin word	Meaning of English word
consumption			
precedence			
biennial			
voluntary			
cogent			
inimical			
ostentation			
perforated			
ignite			
subtraction			

4 *You have already met the verbs in the left-hand column. Give the meanings of the compound verbs:*

traho	subtraho	detraho	extraho	contraho
pello	propello	dispello	compello	repello
fero	differo	defero	circumfero	aufero
verto	reverto	everto	converto	averto
cedo	accedo	intercedo	praecedo	recedo

5 *Here are some military terms derived from words used in Chapters 56–57. Consult your English dictionary and the vocabulary of* **Ecce Romani** *Book 5 to find out how differently the words are used in English and Latin.*

English	Latin	English meaning	Latin meaning
cohort legion legate tribune province impedimenta	cohors legio legatus tribunus provincia impedimenta		

Memoranda

1 *Translate the following quotations which contain verbs in the future perfect tense:*

   (a) cito rumpes arcum, semper si tensum habueris.   (Phaedrus)
   (b) dum loquimur, fugerit invida aetas. carpe diem!   (Horace)
   (c) (eum esse) ingratum si dixeris, omnia dixeris.   (Proverb)
   (d) Domine, memento mei, cum veneris in regnum tuum.   (St Luke 23.42)
   (e) si fueris Romae, Romano vivito more!
      si fueris alibi, vivito sic alibi!   (St Ambrose)

arcus, -us (*m*), bow
tensus, -a, -um, stretched
invidus, -a, -um, envious
aetas, -atis (*f*), age, life

carpo (3), to harvest, enjoy
ingratus, -a, -um, ungrateful, unwelcome
memento! remember!

2 *The following sayings/mottoes contain gerunds:*

   defendendo aggredimur.   (RAF 13 Gunners Squadron)
   exercendo resurgam.   (Medical Rehabilitation Unit)
   ferio ferendo.   (RAF Transport Command)
   findendo fingere disco.   (Institute of Chemical Engineers)

   docendo discimus.   (Proverb)
   arbiter bibendi.   (Horace)
   audendo virtus crescit, tardando timor.   (Lucan)
   crescit scribendo scribendi studium.   (Erasmus)
   dubitando ad verum pervenimus.   (Cicero)

ferio (4), to strike
findo (3), to split, separate
fingo (3), to make, form, fashion

cresco (3), to grow
studium, -i (*n*), enthusiasm, eagerness

3 *Translate the following sayings which contain Gerundives of Obligation:*

nil desperandum.	(family motto)
delenda est Carthago.	(Cato the Elder)
aut ridenda omnia aut flenda sunt.	(Seneca)
adhibenda est in iocando moderatio.	(Cicero)
non ut diu vivamus curandum est sed ut satis.	(Seneca)
de gustibus non disputandum.	(Proverb)
nunc est bibendum, nunc pede libero pulsanda tellus.	(Horace)
bellum nec timendum nec provocandum.	(Pliny)
nox est perpetua una dormienda.	(Catullus)
sed omnes una manet nox et calcanda semel via leti.	(Horace)

est tempus quando nihil, est tempus quando
    aliquid, nullum tamen est tempus in quo dicenda
    sunt omnia.
	(Monk's precept)

adhibeo (2), to summon, employ
curo (1), to trouble oneself about
gustus, -us (*m*), taste

tellus, -uris (*f*), the earth
calco (1), to tread
semel, once
letum, -i (*n*), death

Miranda THE SIBYLLINE BOOKS

Whether or not the Sibylline Books came into the possession of Tarquin in the manner described in Exercenda XIII.4, they certainly existed. They were stored in a stone chest under the Temple of Jupiter Capitolinus, and the privilege of guarding and consulting them was entrusted to a college of priests whose number varied at different periods in Roman history.

At moments of national crisis, as when Hannibal invaded Italy and routed the Romans at the River Trebia, portents seemed to multiply. The historian Livy writes in Book xxii. 62:

"That winter, at Rome and in the neighbourhood of the city, a great many strange things happened or (as is usually the case when people are in a highly suggestive frame of mind) many strange happenings were reported and readily believed.

"For example, a six-month-old child cried out **"io, triumphe!"** in the Vegetable Market; in the Cattle Market, a cow took it into its head to climb up to the third storey of a building from where, startled by the shouting of the tenants, it hurled itself to the ground; an image of ships appeared to shine in the sky; the Temple of Hope in the Vegetable Market was struck by lightning .... On account of these and other portents, the Decemvirs were ordered to consult the books .... First of all, the city was purified ceremonially, great sacrifices of animals were made to the proper gods, a gift of gold weighing forty pounds was carried to the temple of Juno at Lanuvium, the married women dedicated a bronze statue to Juno on the Aventine Hill, ..."

69

So Livy goes on, enumerating the many religious observances which were carried out. He concludes: "All these prayers, sacrifices and acts of piety carried out in accordance with the instructions contained in the Sibylline Books did much to relieve people's minds of superstitious fears."

It required a special decree of the Senate before the priests were allowed to consult the books at all. Only in the desperate kind of situation described by Livy would the Senate be prepared to face the elaborate and costly measures (e.g. the making of statues, the sacrifice of many animals and the erection of massive temples) that the Sibylline Books were sure to prescribe in order to appease the wrath of the gods.

The modern reader may well ask at this point: "What about sceptics like Cicero and Caesar? Did they pay only lip-service to all this mumbo-jumbo? Did they always keep their private reservations to themselves?"

There were, in fact, many sceptics; but, in the many stories told about these unbelievers, their scepticism seems to be their undoing. For example, before engaging the Carthaginians in a naval battle off Sicily in 249 BC, the consul Claudius Pulcher consulted the **pullarius** about the behaviour of the sacred chickens in his charge. When the **pullarius** told him that the chickens had refused their food, Claudius exclaimed, "If they won't eat, let them drink!", and threw them all into the sea. He lost the battle, of course!

Sometimes, a chance remark would so chime in with a particular situation as to suggest an omen without any need of augury. This happened in the case of L. Aemilius Paulus when, in his second consulship, he was given the responsibility of waging war against King Perses of Macedonia.

> "When he returned home in the evening of the very day on which that decision was taken, as he was giving his little daughter a kiss, he noticed that she was on the verge of tears:
> 'What is it, Tertia?' he asked. 'Why are you unhappy?'
> 'Persa is dead, father.'
> Then Paulus gave his daughter a hug and said 'I accept the omen, my daughter.'
> Mind you! It was just a puppy called Persa that had died!"

Cicero discusses the whole subject of augury in his essay "De Divinatione" (from which the above story is taken), and he puts the basic difficulty of all divination quite simply:

> "If the future can have various outcomes, then the future depends entirely on chance; and what is ruled by chance cannot be predetermined. On the other hand, if what is going to happen is determined by fate in every detail of time and circumstance, what help are augurs? Whenever they say that something dreadful is going to happen, they always go on to say that everything will take a turn for the better if we propitiate the gods by religious observances and ceremonies. But, if fate determines everything, there is no point in religious observances . . . . As Homer says, 'What has been preordained is more powerful than all-powerful Jove.'"

Aenigma   Ancient authors

In this puzzle are hidden the English names of 18 Latin authors and one Greek author. At the foot are two famous Latin quotations.

In each box you will find a number. Each number stands for a letter and the same number always represents the same letter. Use the small grid to record the letters as you decipher them. To help you make a start, you are given the numbers for the letters CRY.

When you have deciphered the quotations, you should be able to translate them. *(The solution is on page 144.)*

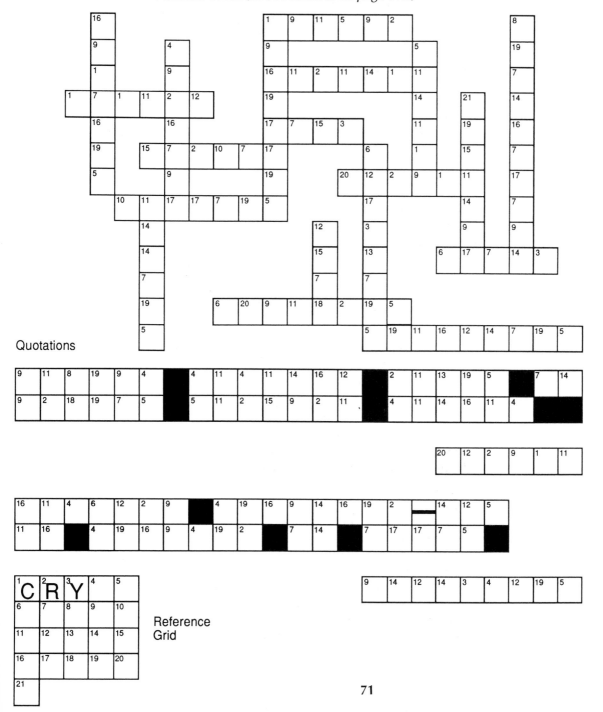

Quotations

Reference Grid

1 C	2 R	3 Y	4	5
6	7	8	9	10
11	12	13	14	15
16	17	18	19	20
21				

Unit XV (Chapters 57–59)

Exercenda 1 *Translate:*

    (a) ubi fures domum intraverunt, magno auxilio mihi fuit hic gladius.

    (b) dux unam legionem praesidio urbi reliquit.

    (c) leones omnibus qui in amphitheatro sedebant magnae admirationi fuerunt.

    (d) haec res magno mihi dedecori fuit.

    (e) dux equites trecentos peditibus subsidio misit.

    (f) amicus meus promisit se auxilio nobis mox venturum esse.

    (g) crudelitas odio est omnibus viris bonis.

    (h) magno bono est hominibus bonam vitam agere.

    (i) mater dixit se hanc pupam filiae dono daturam esse.

    (j) scire volumus cui haec victoria bono fuerit.

    (k) maximae laudi erat consulibus rem publicam contra hostes eo tempore defendisse.

    (l) M. Tullius Cicero consul saluti rei publicae fuit.

2 *Translate:*

    (a) militem iam paenitebat e proelio fugisse.

    (b) diu et ferociter hostibus a custodibus resistebatur.

    (c) ducem oportet nuntiare omnibus captivis parcendum esse.

    (d) ubi ad flumen perventum est, militibus licuit quietem unius diei capere.

    (e) consuli persuasum est ut exercitum ad urbem statim reduceret.

    (f) legatis pacem petentibus nihil responsum est.

    (g) si mihi parebitur, captivis parcetur.

    (h) cum copiae hostium visae essent, ex agris in urbem undique concursum est.

    (i) quamquam dixerunt se innocentes esse, eis non credetur.

    (j) quod illum pudet crudelitatis, cives decet ei veniam dare.

    (k) cum nuntiatum esset arcem captam esse, militibus imperatum est ut arma statim deponerent.

    (l) si te ipsum regi trades, tuis liberis non nocebitur.

3 *Translate:*

Second Invasion of Britain

accessum est ad Britanniam omnibus navibus meridiano fere tempore, neque in eo loco hostis est visus;   sed, ut postea Caesar ex captivis cognovit, cum magnae manus eo convenissent, multitudine navium perterritae, quae amplius octingentae uno tempore erant
5 visae, a litore discesserant ac se in superiora loca abdiderant.

Caesar, exposito exercitu et loco castris idoneo capto, ubi ex captivis cognovit quo in loco hostium copiae consedissent, cohortibus decem ad mare relictis et equitibus trecentis qui praesidio navibus essent, de tertia vigilia ad hostes contendit, eo minus veritus
10 navibus quod in litore molli atque aperto deligatas ad ancoram relinquebat;   et praesidio navibus Q. Atrium praefecit.

ipse, noctu progressus milia passuum circiter XII, hostium copias conspicatus est.   illi, equitatu atque essedis ad flumen progressi, ex loco superiore nostros prohibere et proelium committere coeperunt.
15 repulsi ab equitatu se in silvas abdiderunt, locum nacti egregie et natura et opere munitum, quem domestici belli causa iam ante praeparaverant;   nam crebris arboribus succisis omnes introitus erant praeclusi.   ipsi ex silvis rari propugnabant nostrosque intra munitiones ingredi prohibebant.   at milites legionis septimae,
20 testudine facta et aggere ad munitiones adiecto, locum ceperunt eosque ex silvis expulerunt paucis vulneribus acceptis.

sed eos fugientes longius Caesar prosequi vetuit, et quod loci naturam ignorabat et quod, magna parte diei consumpta, munitioni castrorum tempus relinqui volebat.

Caesar, Bellum Gallicum V. 8–9

A testudo

accedo (3), **-cessi, -cessum,** to approach	**nanciscor** (3), **nactus sum,** to obtain
meridiano fere tempore, about mid-day	**egregie,** excellently, very well
manus, -us (*f*), band	**opus, operis** (*n*), work
amplius, more	**creber, -bra, -brum,** many, numerous
abdo (3), **abdidi, abditum,** to hide	**succido** (3), **-cidi, -cisum,** to cut down, fell
qui praesidio essent (+ *dat.*), to guard	**introitus, -us** (*m*), entrance
contendo (3), **-di, -tum,** to hasten	**praecludo** (3), **-clusi, -clusum,** to block
eo minus veritus navibus, being less anxious about the ships	**rarus, -a, -um,** here and there, intermittently
litus, -oris (*n*), beach, shore	**propugno** (1), to rush out to fight
mollis, -is, -e, gentle	**adicio** (3), **-ieci, -iectum,** to throw up, build near
praeficio (3), **-feci, -fectum,** to put in command	

4 *Do not translate unless asked to do so, but answer in English the questions which follow the passage:*

Shame or Honour?

L. Manlio Volsone et M. Atilio Regulo consulibus, bellum in Africam translatum est.   nam Hamilcar, Carthaginiensis dux, pugna maritima victus exercitum domum reduxit.   consules, cum in Africam transiissent, ad Carthaginem processerunt.   in urbem
5 tamen impetum nondum fecerunt sed primum vicinas gentes superare constituerunt.   multis oppidis deletis, Manlius victor

Romam cum magna parte exercitus a senatu revocatus est ut comitia in proximum annum haberet.

Regulus in Africa remansit, Carthaginem ipsam capturus.   primo
10 rem bene gessit, nam contra tres Carthaginiensium duces pugnans victor fuit.   tum Carthaginienses animo deiecti pacem a Romanis petierunt.   quam cum Regulus nollet dare nisi duris condicionibus, Carthaginienses auxilium a Lacedaemoniis petierunt;   et duce Xanthippo qui a Lacedaemoniis missus erat, Regulum vicerunt
15 maxima pernicie.   nam duo milia tantum ex omni Romano exercitu refugere poterant;   quingenti cum imperatore Regulo capti sunt; XXX milia occisa.   Regulus ipse in catenas est coniectus.   non iam pacem petierunt Carthaginienses;   mox quidem Romanos proelio superabant.
20   sex post annis tamen L. Caecilius Metellus consul Carthaginienses in Sicilia superavit.   viginti milibus hostium occisis, reliquos captos cum XXVI elephantis Romam victor deduxit.   iterum pacem petere constituerunt Carthaginienses.

Regulum Romam miserunt qui pacem a Romanis obtineret ac
25 permutationem captivorum faceret.   consentiebat Regulus, si haec agere non posset, se Carthaginem rediturum esse.   ille Romam cum venisset, inductus in senatum nihil quasi Romanus egit.   dixit enim se ex illo die, quo ab hostibus captus esset, Romanum esse desiisse. itaque et uxorem ab amplexu removit et Romanos hortatus est ne
30 pax cum Poenis fieret.   affirmavit enim se tanti non esse ut tot milia captivorum propter se et paucos, qui ex Romanis capti erant, redderentur.   itaque obtinuit, nam Carthaginienses pacem petentes nemo admisit.

ipse Carthaginem rediit;   offerentibusque Romanis ut eum
35 Romae tenerent, negavit se in ea urbe mansurum esse in qua, postquam Poenis servierat, dignitatem honesti civis habere non posset.   regressus igitur ad Africam omnibus suppliciis exstinctus est.

Eutropius II, 21

comitia, -orum (n.pl), elections
in proximum annum, for the following year
rem bene gessit, (he) was successful
animo deiecti, demoralised
pernicies, -ei (f), destruction, losses
catenae, -arum (f.pl), chains
obtineo (2), -tinui, -tentum, to obtain, have one's way
permutatio, -onis (f), exchange

consentio (4), -sensi, -sensum, to agree
desino, -ere (3), desii, to cease
Poeni, -orum (m.pl), Carthaginians
tanti esse, to be so valuable
admitto (3), -misi, -missum, to give an audience to
servio (4) (+dat.), to be a slave (to)
dignitas, -atis (f), status
honestus, -a, -um, honourable, respected
supplicium, -i (n), punishment, torture

(i) Comprehension Questions:

(a) By what methods does the author identify the years in which the events occurred?

(b) List, in chronological order, the six events which are mentioned in the first paragraph.

(c) What is the tense of **capturus** (line 9)? Why was this tense used?

(d) To what word does **quam** (line 12) refer?

(e) What was the decisive factor in bringing about Regulus' defeat after his initial successes?

(f) How long was Regulus a prisoner of the Carthaginians before his return to Rome?

(g) What two things was Regulus told to arrange?

(h) What reason did Regulus give for his actions/advice in lines 27–32?

(i) Where were the prisoners to whom the words **tot milia** refer? (line 30); and to whom does the word **paucos** (line 31) refer?

(j) What was the ultimate fate of Regulus?

(ii) Discussion Points:

(a) What reason did Regulus give for rejecting the offer made in line 34?

(b) Eutropius obviously wished to emphasise how important honour was to a Roman. By means of two examples drawn from lines 24–38, show how Regulus put honour before personal advantage.

(c) Why do you think Regulus agreed to go to Rome (**consentiebat**, line 25) when he had no intention of doing what the Carthaginians ordered?

(d) Quote the Latin words in the last paragraph which mean roughly "he couldn't hold his head up high".

(e) Do you think that the words **nihil quasi Romanus egit** (line 27) are intended by the author as a compliment or criticism of Regulus? Give reasons for your answer.

Derivanda

1 *List the Latin words from which the English words are derived and give the meanings of the Latin and the English words:*

English word	*Latin word*	*Meaning of Latin word*	*Meaning of English word*
aperture diffidence pedestrian contact valetudinarian salutary adhesive recession precept			

2 *In the first column, there is a list of Latin words about "ships" and the
"sea". In the second column, write down as many English derivatives as
possible from each of these:*

Latin word	English derivatives
mare, maris (*n*) **maritimus, -a, -um** **fluctus, -us** (*m*) **unda, -ae** (*f*) **navis, -is** (*f*) **navigo** (1) **portus, -us** (*m*) **tempestas, -atis** (*f*) **insula, -ae** (*f*) **aqua, -ae** (*f*)	

3 *Revision of earlier exercises:*

*(a) The suffix "-ine" means "pertaining to, in the nature of". Give the
meaning of:*

feline   porcine   elephantine   aquiline
feminine   asinine   taurine   leonine

*(b) The suffix "-ile" has two basic meanings: "having the characteristics
of" and "capable of". Give the meanings of:*

   (i) virile, juvenile, senile, puerile;
   (ii) fertile, reptile, mobile, docile, versatile, tactile, prehensile, missile.

*(c) The Latin suffix "-osus", meaning "full of", becomes "-ose" or
"-ous" in English. From the Latin words give English derivatives and
their meanings:*

Latin word + meaning	English word	Meaning of English word
spatiosus bellicosus odiosus iocosus copiosus pretiosus verbosus famosus periculosus		

(d) The suffix "-fy" means "to make". Give the meanings of:

satisfy   nullify   sanctify   solidify   stupefy
liquefy   vilify   mollify   rarefy   unify

*(e) The Latin verb suffix **-sco** means "grow" or "become". Find the meanings of these words in your English dictionary:*

fluorescent	effervescent	quiescent	evanescent
putrescent	adolescent	obsolescent	senescent

4 *Some Latin expressions are now in common usage in English. Use your knowledge of Latin to work out what the following mean:*

(a) Although you do not like the new manager, it is desirable to establish a **modus operandi** with him.

(b) We cannot discuss that case because it is still **sub judice**.

(c) The diplomat was declared **persona non grata** and ordered to leave the country.

(d) You are not legally entitled to compensation for the loss of your valuables, but we are prepared to make you an **ex gratia** payment.

(e) The Latin words **Requiescat in Pace,** or its abbreviated form R.I.P., can often be seen on tombstones.

(f) The scientist, **qua** scientist, cannot be held responsible for the later misuse of his discovery.

(g) Since the proposal was uncontroversial, it was accepted by the committee, **nem con**.

Memoranda

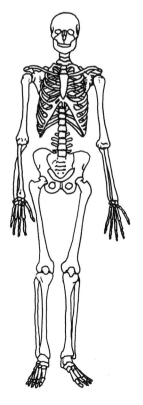

I. SCIENTIFIC LATIN

Latin continues to be used and to have its use continually extended in the biological sciences:

(a) Anatomy. The main bones of the skeleton have Latin names, and many of these have been incorporated into layman's English, e.g.

Latin word	*Normal Latin meaning*	*Anatomical meaning*
radius	staff, rod	outer forearm bone
ulna	elbow	larger forearm bone
humerus	upper arm, shoulder	upper arm bone
clavicula	little bolt	collar-bone
scapula	shoulder-blade	shoulder-blade
vertebrae	joints	joints of backbone
costa	rib	rib
pelvis	basin	cavity for kidneys
femur	thigh	thigh bone
patella	little plate	knee-cap
tibia	flute	shinbone
fibula	clasp	outer bone between knee and ankle

Try to identify the above bones in the accompanying diagram.

(b) Botany. All plants have international Latin names so that they may be identified world-wide. The vocabulary of such words is immense, and many of the words used are not familiar to most readers of Latin. However, the adjectives which accompany these nouns are often very descriptive.

For example, **carex** is the Latin word for "reed-grass" or "rush".

From your knowledge of Latin, what information can you deduce about the following reeds?

carex alpina	carex humilis	carex pendula
carex diversicolor	carex maritima	carex rigida
carex elongata	carex nigra	carex montana
carex gracilis	carex sylvatica	carex rariflora

NATURE CONSERVATION
17P
SPECIES AT RISK
BARN OWL
(TYTO ALBA)

(Reproduction by permission of Post Office Letters)

(c) Ornithology. Here again, Latin words are used to describe accurately the various species of birds, e.g.

corvus, -i (*m*), crow   **passer, -eris** (*m*), sparrow
anser, -eris (*m*), goose   **turdus, -i** (*m*), thrush

Here too, adjectives are often descriptive, e.g.

anser albifrons   passer domesticus
anser fabalis ("fond of beans")   passer montanus

In naming birds, ornithologists often use three terms which stand for

(i) *genus*, i.e. the name for the whole family. (**genus, generis** (*n*), origin, class, kind)
(ii) *species*, i.e. a particular group within the genus. (**species, -ei** (*f*) means "appearance"; a particular "quality" which distinguishes one group from another)
(iii) *sub-species*, i.e. a sub-division of the species.

Sometimes the second word is repeated, i.e. where a bird of a particular sub-species is also the typical member of the species, e.g.

turdus merula merula   Blackbird
turdus musicus musicus   Continental Song Thrush
turdus torquatus torquatus   Ring-ousel

     merula, -ae (*f*), blackbird
     torquatus, -a, -um, adorned with a collar

Occasionally, the same word appears three times, i.e. where the bird is the typical member of the genus, the species and the sub-species, e.g.

riparia riparia riparia   Sandmartin
oriolus oriolus oriolus   Golden Oriole

     riparius, -a, -um, frequenting the banks of rivers

II. LATIN IN THE HOSPITAL

There are many medical words derived from Latin, including the
following:

* ambulance	**ambulare,** to walk
amputate	**amputare,** to cut off
ancillary	**ancilla,** maidservant
auxiliary	**auxilium,** help
casualty	**casus,** chance, fall
consultant	**consultare,** to consult
convalescent	**convalescere,** to grow well
dislocate	**dis + locare,** to place apart
doctor	**doctus,** skilled
fracture	**frangere (fractum),** to break
hospital	**hospitium,** guest-house
incubator	**in** ("in") **+ cubare,** to lie
infirmary	**infirmus,** weak
injection	**inicere (iniectum),** to thrust in
inoculate	**in** ("into") **+ oculus** ("eye, bud"), to put a "bud" into
invalid	**invalidus,** weak
matron	**matrona,** lady (of rank)
medicine	**medicus,** doctor
operation	**opera,** work
patient	**patiens,** suffering
pulse	**pulsare,** to beat
respirator	**respirare,** to breathe
resuscitate	**resuscitare,** to revive (**re + sub + citare**)
transfusion	**transfundere (-fusum),** to pour from one vessel to another
vaccinate	**vacca,** cow

 * Contracted from the French *hôpital ambulant*, "a moving hospital".

Miranda   THE STORY OF THE LATIN LANGUAGE 1

The problem of how language itself began is probably insoluble, though
that fact has not prevented scholars from making intelligent guesses
about its origin. Another fascinating problem about languages is
this: "Why are there so many languages and why are they all different?"

For a time, no one could find a solution to this riddle either. The writer
of the Book of Genesis conceived of this multiplicity of languages as a
punishment by God of man's pride; and so it was widely believed until
about the end of the eighteenth century when Sanskrit, which had been
preserved in the Hindu religious writings of India, became known to

Western scholars through the work of Sir William Jones. He noticed that Sanskrit closely resembled words in other languages, e.g.

English	German	Latin	Greek	Sanskrit
mother	Mutter	mater	μητηε	matar
two	zwei	duo	δυο	dvau

It became suddenly apparent that Latin, Greek and Sanskrit were sister-languages; and further investigation soon showed that behind languages like Russian, German and Gaelic lay shadowy ancestors of equal antiquity with Sanskrit, all showing a common core of vocabulary and common linguistic habits.

The next step was to suppose that all these languages had a common parent; on the grounds that languages from both India and Europe stemmed from this hypothetical parent-language, it was given the title "Indo-European." (See diagram opposite.)

In earlier exercises in these Companion Books we have traced some of the ways in which Latin has remained persistently alive in the vocabularies of its daughter-languages. The following table illustrates the close kinship in the vocabulary of the principal Romance languages, "Romance" being the generic term for Latin-based languages:

English	Latin	French	Spanish	Portuguese	Italian	Rumanian
all	totus	tout	todo	todo	tutto	tot
come	venire	venir	venir	vir	venire	veni
do	facere	faire	hacer	fazer	fare	face
gold	aurum	or	oro	auro	oro	aur
good	bonus	bon	bueno	bom	buono	bun
green	viridis	vert	verde	verde	verde	verde
king	rex	roi	rey	rei	re	rege

The curious thing about the above list is the fact that the words in the English column do not appear to be related to the words in the other columns. As Rome extended its empire, Latin not only ousted other similar languages (e.g. Oscan and Umbrian) from the Italian peninsula but also supplanted the native Celtic tongues of Gaul, the Iberian peninsula and Dacia (modern Rumania). However, this did not happen in Britain where the native population continued to be Celtic-speaking during the Roman occupation. When the occupation ended, it was the Germanic language of the invading Anglo-Saxons that took over. The Celts retreated into Cornwall, Wales, Ireland and the highlands and islands of Scotland, where their tongues have survived to the present day.

The basic vocabulary of English comes from the Germanic branch of Indo-European, as the following list shows:

English :	all	come	do	gold	good	green	king
German :	alle	kommen	tun	Gold	gut	grün	König

To the basic Germanic foundation was added a superstructure of Romance vocabulary through two later influences — the Norman Conquest and the Roman Catholic Church. The former introduced French words of Latin origin, the latter used Latin in its services. These different influences have given English a rich and flexible vocabulary. The following lists indicate some of these derivations, and also some of the variations of meaning and form that have developed:

WORDS DERIVED FROM LATIN		WORDS OF SIMILAR MEANING FROM GERMANIC SOURCE
Straight from Latin	Through French	
rex, regis regal	royal	kingly
computare compute	count	reckon
securus secure	sure	steady
iratus irate	—	angry
cadere cadence	chance	fall
directus direct	adroit	straight
focus focus	foyer	hearth
implicare implicate	employ(ment)	work
replicare replicate replica	reply	answer
explicare explicit	exploit	deed
(Supine: **explicitum**)		

Heavy frames indicate parent languages which no longer exist.

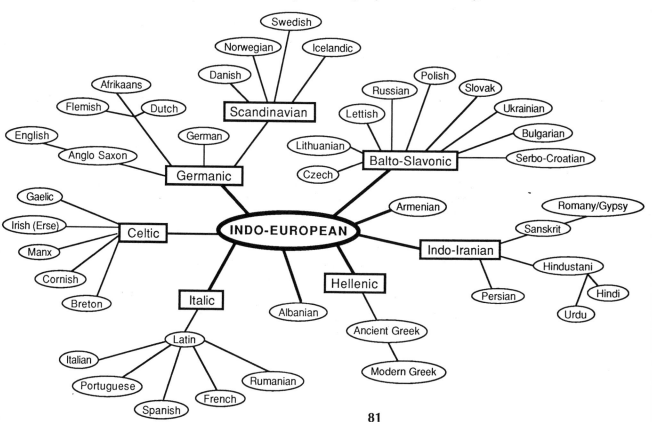

81

Aenigma   A Military Word Search

The 41 words all appear in straight lines (horizontal, vertical or diagonal) but never backwards. The same letters may be used in more than one word.

The solution is on page 144.

	a	b	c	d	e	f	g	h	i	j	k	l	m	n
1	S	C	L	C	A	L	I	G	A	E	A	C	P	L
2	C	A	E	V	A	C	I	E	S	L	R	O	U	E
3	A	G	G	E	R	Q	F	V	Q	T	M	H	G	G
4	L	M	I	L	E	S	U	S	I	U	A	O	I	A
5	A	E	O	C	A	R	N	I	N	T	E	R	O	T
6	E	N	L	E	E	D	D	G	L	V	I	S	H	U
7	B	S	O	N	E	N	I	A	R	I	E	S	I	S
8	A	A	C	T	E	S	T	U	D	O	F	A	B	B
9	L	G	A	U	I	G	O	U	S	P	E	E	E	R
10	L	U	G	R	T	D	R	H	R	L	I	I	R	A
11	I	L	R	I	T	U	B	A	A	I	R	L	N	C
12	S	U	I	A	C	X	M	G	A	B	O	D	A	A
13	T	M	L	E	G	I	O	N	A	R	I	U	S	E
14	A	O	N	A	G	E	R	F	O	S	S	A	L	A

dagger
boots
tortoise
cohort
javelins
marching column
line of battle
sword
winter quarters
skill
territory
helmet
2 catapults

ditch
engineers
ladders
standard
battering ram
weapons
shield
tower
leather trousers
force
wing
trumpet
centurion's staff

centurion
century
military cloak
legion
legionary soldier (2 words)
cavalryman
their own men
legionary commander
slinger
places
general
standard bearer
rampart

Unit XVI (Chapters 60–74)

Exercenda

1 *Translate:*

(a) si id sentit, cur nobis non dixit?

(b) nisi Brundisium festinabis, amici tui sine te navem solvent.

(c) si ulla spes esset urbis defendendae, vos non monerem ut effugeretis.

(d) si audiant quid acciderit, nobis numquam auxilio veniant.

(e) nisi Cicero scelera Catilinae patefecisset, res publica eversa esset.

(f) si pater tuus adhuc viveret, nemo e servis matrem tuam sic alloqui auderet.

(g) si negavit se nocentem esse, cur ei non credis?

(h) nisi Caesar Helvetios Rhodanum transire prohibuisset, illi totam provinciam occupavissent.

(i) si eum Romam arcessam, ei non placeat.

(j) si hostes aquilam cepissent, id maximo dedecori legioni fuisset.

2 *Translate:*

(a) dona ad eum remittantur; timeo enim ne nos furti accuset.

(b) ne comites in hoc tanto rerum discrimine deseramus.

(c) imperator, veritus ne naves longae tempestate delerentur, nautas vetuit navem solvere.

(d) Romae paulo diutius commoremur ut ad ludos in Circo habitos eamus.

(e) iter equo faciant quo celerius ad villam perveniant.

(f) ne timeamus vera semper dicere.

(g) taceas, Marce, ne quis te talia dicentem audiat!

(h) viatores verebantur ne sibi non parceretur nisi praedoni pecuniam tradidissent.

(i) ne umquam negent se esse Romanos.

(j) utinam eam hortatus essem ut domum rediret ut patri morienti valediceret.

utinam, I wish that

3 *Translate:*

Maximus Valerius Corvinus

de Maximo Valerio, qui Corvinus appellatus est ob auxilium propugnationemque corvi, haec res miranda in libris annalibus est memorata.

L. Furio, Claudio Appio consulibus, adulescens fit tribunus
5 militaris.   atque in eo tempore copiae Gallorum ingentes agrum Pomptinum insederant, instruebaturque acies a consulibus.   dux interea Gallorum, vasta proceritate armisque auro fulgentibus,

manu telum reciprocans incedebat;   perque contemptum et
superbiam circumspiciens despiciensque omnia, venire iubet et
10   congredi, si quis pugnare secum ex omni Romano exercitu auderet.
    tum Valerius tribunus, ceteris inter metum pudoremque ambiguis,
impetrato prius a consulibus ut in Gallum arrogantem pugnare sese
permitterent, progreditur intrepide obviam.   et congrediuntur et
consistunt et conserebantur iam manus.   atque ibi vis quaedam
15   divina fit.
    corvus repente improvisus advolat et super galeam tribuni insistit,
atque inde in adversarii os atque oculos pugnare incipit;   insiliebat,
obturbabat et unguibus manum laniabat et prospectum alis arcebat.
atque, ubi satis saevierat, revolabat in galeam tribuni.   sic tribunus,
20   spectante utroque exercitu, et sua virtute nixus et opera corvi
propugnatus, ducem hostium ferocissimum vicit interfecitque;
atque ob hanc causam cognomen habuit Corvinus.   id factum
est annis quadringentis quinque post Romam conditam.
    statuam Corvino isti divus Augustus in foro suo statuendam
25   curavit.   in eius statuae capite corvi simulacrum est, rei pugnaeque
quam diximus monumentum.

Aulus Gellius, IX.11

propugnatio, -onis (*f*), defence,
    protection
corvus, -i (*m*), raven
libri annales, archives, records
memoro (1), to relate
proceritas, -atis (*f*), height
fulgeo (2), **fulsi,** to shine, flash,
    gleam
reciproco (1), to brandish
incedo (3), **-cessi, -cessum,** to
    strut about
pudor, -oris (*m*), shame
ambiguus, -a, -um, wavering
impetrato, having had his
    request granted
manum conserere, to engage in
    hand-to-hand fighting

improvisus, -a, -um,
    unexpected(ly)
insisto (3), **institi,** to settle on,
    alight
obturbo (1), to confuse, distract
unguis, -is (*m*), talon
lanio (1), to tear at
ala, -ae (*f*), wing
arceo (2), to obstruct
saevio (4), to vent one's rage
nixus (+ *abl.*), relying (upon)
opera, -ae (*f*), work, efforts
divus, -a, -um, deified
curo (1), to arrange for

4   *Before tackling this passage, pupils should study the notes on Medieval
Latin on page 223 of* **Ecce Romani** *Book 5.*

The Faithful Dog

*A soldier has squandered his inheritance and is now living from hand to
mouth in a foreign city.*

mansit ergo miles in civitate cibos cottidie cane vel accipitre querens,
quia non aliud habebat unde viveret.   ibat igitur cottidie venari,
uxore domi ieiuna manente dum ille rediens leporem aut gruem aut
tale aliquid detulisset.   si vero redisset vacuus, usque ad diei
5   sequentis vesperam ieiunebant, vel dum ille cepisset aliquid.

contigit autem ut quadam die nihil venatione caperet; sequenti
mane, adhuc ab heri ieiunus, cane domi relicto, cum accipitre et
equo cibum quesitum ivit.   porro illo diutius morante, uxor eius
biduanam famem non sustinens coacta est domum egredi
10 matroneque cuiusdam intrare hospicium ut cibum rogaret.
  interim autem, dum ista in domo matrone, ille vero in venatione
esset, serpens immanis de caverna muri prodiens parvulum, qui
domi remanserat, interimere aggressus est.   quod cum videret
canis, cathenam qua ligatus est rupit pugnamque iniit cum serpente.
15 quo victo et interfecto, dentibus ipsum longius a parvulo traxit.   in
conflictu autem cunabulum fuerat versum, ita ut vultus parvuli
respiceret pavimentum.
  ecce autem statim miles, capta preda rediens, intravit domum
viditque versum cunabulum, cruentatum canem totumque infectum
20 sanguine pavimentum.   arbitrans igitur canem fame coactum
parvulum devorasse, uxorem fugisse, in impetu ire canem gladio
trucidavit.   cum vero et se ipsum gladio extinguere vellet, venit
uxor erectoque rursum cunabulo filium lactavit.   tunc et serpentem
interfectum reperierunt fidemque canis intuentur.   penitet
25 commissi militem, sed sero.

The Story of the Seven Wise Men

accipiter, -tris (*m*), hawk
querens = quaerens
ieiunus, -a, -um, not having
  eaten, without food
dum, until
lepus, -oris (*m*), hare
grus, gruis (*f*), crane
vacuus, -a, -um, empty-handed
vespera, -ae (*f*), evening
contigit ut, it happened that
quesitum ire, to go to look for
porro, far off
biduanam famem, the two-day
  hunger
hospicium, -i (*n*), home
parvulus, -i (*m*), baby

interimo (3), **-emi, -emptum,** to
  kill
cathena = catena
ligo (1), to tie
cunabula, -orum (*n.pl*), cradle
pavimentum, -i (*n*), floor
cruentatus, -a, -um, covered in
  blood
ire = irae
trucido (1), to kill (cruelly)
rursum, again
lacto (1), to feed with milk, suckle
reperio (4), to find
intueor (2), to see, observe
commissum, -i (*n*), action, deed

5 *Do not translate unless asked to do so, but answer in English the questions which follow:*

The exiled Roman Coriolanus leads the enemy against Rome

tum matronae ad Veturiam, matrem Coriolani, Volumniamque
uxorem frequentes coeunt.   oraverunt ut Veturia et Volumnia duos
parvos ferens filios secum in castra hostium irent et, quoniam armis
viri defendere urbem non possent, mulieres precibus lacrimisque
5 defenderent.
    ubi ad castra ventum est nuntiatumque Coriolano est adesse
ingens mulierum agmen, primo Coriolanus, qui nec maiestate
legatorum nec sacerdotum religione motus erat, multo obstinatior
adversus lacrimas muliebres erat.   deinde amicorum quidam, qui
10 cognoverat Volumniam inter ceteras stantem, "nisi me decipiunt"
inquit "oculi, mater tibi uxorque et liberi adsunt."
    cum Coriolanus sollicitus ab sede sua descendisset ad matrem
complectendam, mulier in iram ex precibus conversa "antequam
complexus tuos accipio," inquit "volo scire utrum ad hostem an ad
15 filium venerim, utrum captiva an mater in castris tuis sim.   ad hoc
me traxit longa vita ut te exulem deinde hostem viderem?   potuisti
populari hanc terram quae te genuit atque aluit?   cum in conspectu
Roma fuit, nonne tibi in mentem venit: 'intra illa moenia domus et
penates mei sunt, mater coniunx liberique'?   nisi ego te
20 peperissem, Roma non oppugnaretur;   nisi filium haberem, libera
in libera patria mortua essem."
    uxor deinde ac liberi amplexi fletusque ab omni turba mulierum
ortus fregerunt tandem virum.   complexus inde suos dimittit;   ipse
retro ab urbe castra movit.

Livy, Book II.40

frequentes, in large numbers	**gigno** (3), **genui, genitum,** to give
preces, -um (*f.pl*), prayers,	birth to
entreaties	**alo** (3), **alui, altum,** to nourish
maiestas, -atis (*f*), majesty,	**moenia, -ium** (*n.pl*), walls
dignity	**penates, -ium** (*m.pl*), house-
sacerdos, -otis (*m*), priest	hold gods
religio, -onis (*f*), awe, reverence	**pario** (3), **peperi, partum,** to bear
adversus (+ *acc.*), in response	(a child)
to, faced with	**patria, -ae** (*f*), native land
muliebris, -is, -e, of a woman	**fletus, -us** (*m*), weeping
exul, exulis (*m*), exile	**complector** (3), **-plexus sum,** to
populor (1), **-atus sum,** to	embrace
plunder, ravage	**sui, suorum** (*m.pl*), his relations
	retro, back

(i) Comprehension Questions:

(a) What was the relationship between Veturia and Volumnia?

(b) With what "weapons" were the women to defend the city?

(c) What other attempts had been made to persuade Coriolanus to withdraw his forces?

(d) What was Coriolanus' initial reaction to the arrival of the women?

(e) What changed his attitude and how did he then behave?

(f) Translate **nisi ego . . . mortua essem** (lines 19–21).

(ii) Discussion Points:

(a) Veturia put five questions to Coriolanus. In what way did the first two differ from the three others? What effect were the last three intended to have on Coriolanus?

(b) According to the author, what two things persuaded Coriolanus to withdraw?

(c) What else do you think might have been responsible for his withdrawal?

(d) A true Roman would normally have responded to both **maiestas legatorum** and **sacerdotum religio** (lines 7–8), but these phrases would have appealed to different sides of his character. What were these?

Derivanda

1 *Find the meanings of the following English words associated with the law, the courts, etc:*

(a) From **lex, legis** (*f*), law:

legal	legislator	legitimate
legality	legislature	illegal

(b) From **iudex, iudicis** (*m*), judge:

judicial	judgment	judicature
judicious	adjudicate	judiciary

(c) From **ius, iuris** (*n*), law, right:

jury	juror	jurist
juridical	jurisdiction	jurisprudence

(d) From **iuro** (1), to take an oath, swear:

adjure   abjure   perjure   conjure

2 *The Latin ending* **-arius** *describes "a person who does something".*

(a) Give the Latin word for the man who

(i) drives a carriage	(raeda)	(iv) fights wild beasts	(bestia)
(ii) carries a litter	(lectica)	(v) uses a dagger	(sica)
(iii) delivers letters	(tabella)	(vi) works with silver	(argentum)

(b) What would the following do?

(i) retiarius	(v) legionarius
(ii) essedarius	(vi) aquarius
(iii) falcarius	(vii) adversarius
(iv) pullarius	(viii) sagittarius

3 *The Latin diphthong* -ae *often becomes* -e *in English derivatives. Using this information, produce one or more English word(s) derived from each of the following, and relate the meaning of the English word to that of the Latin word.*

praemium	aequalis	praecedo
caelestis	praeceps, -ipitis	praescribo
aeternus	praefero	praesens, -ntis
haesito	paenitentia	adhaereo

4 *The following exercises provide revision practice. Complete the columns:*

(a)

Latin noun + meaning	English noun	Meaning of English word
lassitudo		
turpitudo		
pulchritudo		
amplitudo		
solitudo		
similitudo		

(b)

brevitas		
iniquitas		
alacritas		
facultas		
societas		
necessitas		
securitas		
claritas		
nobilitas		
atrocitas		

(c)

scientia		
prudentia		
temperantia		
ignorantia		
diligentia		
patientia		
paenitentia		
eloquentia		

5 *Use your knowledge of Latin to work out the meanings of these English words. Note especially the prefixes and Latin stems.*

English word	Prefix(es)	Other Latin word(s)	Meaning of English word
circumlocution superimpose coincidence introspective decapitate intermediary exculpate extrovert introvert internecine	circum	loquor	

6 *Work out the meanings of the Latin phrases in the following sentences:*

    (a) When the body was found, **rigor mortis** had already set in.

    (b) The doctor will employ a **locum (tenens)** while she is on holiday.

    (c) The Chairman of the Council is **ex officio** a member of all Council committees.

    (d) The British government gave immediate **de facto** though not **de iure** recognition to the island's new government.

    (e) In detective stories, the first question often asked after a murder is "**cui bono?**"

    (f) The **interim** secretary will handle all correspondence until a permanent secretary can be appointed.

    (g) Sometimes a list of **corrigenda** or **errata** is inserted at the beginning of a book.

    (h) "My lazy son has, **mirabile dictu**, passed his exams", said the father.

7 *Many Latin loan words become more specialised in meaning when they are transferred to English. Copy out and complete the following table, using a dictionary if necessary.*

Latin	Meaning of word in Latin	English word	Meaning of word in English
onus	burden, load	onus	
opus	piece of work	opus	
genus	type, kind	genus	
regimen	guidance	regimen	
candor	brilliant whiteness	candour	
splendor	brightness	splendour	
vapor	steam	vapour	
cantor	singer	cantor	
monitor	adviser	monitor	
rabies	madness	rabies	
educator	foster-father	educator	
tutor	guardian	tutor	

Memoranda   I. LATIN IN THE CONCERT HALL

The casual newspaper reader who comes upon advertisements for forthcoming musical concerts must often be puzzled by their terms of reference. Orchestral items, it is true, can usually be put into general categories like symphony and concerto; but the field of choral music seems to abound in cryptic Latin titles such as Monteverdi's "Magnificat", Cavalli's "Laudate Dominum" and Vivaldi's "Gloria." Concert promoters seem to assume that, having been given the first word or phrase, the music enthusiast will be able to supply the rest of the Latin text.

This may seem a large assumption, but the Latin text is in many instances quite short, and the first word does provide a reliable clue as to how the text will continue. For instance, the word "Magnificat" always refers to the hymn of the Virgin, to be found in St Luke Chapter 1, verses 46–55, and beginning "My soul doth magnify the Lord" (**Magnificat anima mea Dominum**). Again, what is known as the "Agnus Dei" consists simply of the words **Agnus Dei, qui tollis peccata mundi, miserere nobis, dona nobis pacem.**

Although these musical works can be very long, the Latin text on which they are all based is quite short. The composer uses manifold repetition, the same phrases being picked up over and over again in various ways. The power of such musical settings depends upon the skilful combination of the sounds of the Latin words and the accentual patterns of the music. Indeed, the Latin sounds are often integral to the very effect the composer is aiming at. Compare, for instance, the Latin of a stanza from the "Dies Irae" with the alternative English as printed in the vocal score of Verdi's "Requiem":

Confutatis maledictis	When the cursed all are banished,
Flammis acribus addictis	Doomed to that devouring furnace,
Voca me cum benedictis.	Summon me among the blessed.

The translator has, admittedly, produced a version which can be sung — just! But the triple rhyme has gone, and so too has the harsh sequence of d's, t's and s's which so powerfully reinforce Verdi's terrifying musical picture of the Day of Judgment. Small wonder that Latin is always retained in performance!

From the earliest days of the Christian Church, all the worshippers took part in singing "hymns and . . . spiritual songs", as Paul puts it; and, as Christian worship developed a more formal pattern, the Latin hymns and sentences for congregational use settled down into a standard sequence.

However, worshippers are not necessarily musicians, and it was probably to lead the congregational singing that choirs were formed initially. Then, when church musicians found that they had a body of trained singers at their disposal, they began to make elaborate musical settings of the texts specifically for their choirs — not as a series of separate items spread through a church service, but as a continuous musical work suitable for transplanting from church to concert hall. The sequence of texts used in the celebration of Mass in church was "Kyrie, Gloria, Credo, Sanctus (including the Benedictus), Agnus Dei." Any musical work using this sequence is therefore known as a mass even though it is intended purely for concert performance, e.g. Bach's B Minor Mass and Beethoven's Mass in D.

The most dramatic form of the mass, and the one which has arguably inspired the greatest music, is the Requiem Mass, a prayer that the dead person's soul may rest in peace. Again, it is normal to use only the first word of the text when referring to these, e.g. The Requiem of Verdi, Fauré or Mozart.

The more joyful parts of the normal mass are omitted, such as the "Gloria" and "Credo" (The Creed); and some parts, or even the whole, of the thirteenth-century Latin poem called the "Dies Irae", which deals with the terrors of the Day of Judgment, are included, producing the following sequence:

(1) INTROIT:

Requiem aeternam dona eis, Domine, et lux perpetua luceat eis!
Grant them eternal peace, Lord, and may your perpetual light shine upon them!

(2) KYRIE (the only Greek Section of the Mass):

Kyrie eleison!   Christe eleison!   Kyrie eleison!
Lord, have mercy! Christ, have mercy! Lord, have mercy!

(3) DIES IRAE

(4) SANCTUS:

Sanctus, sanctus, sanctus, Dominus Deus Sabaoth*   *(Sabaoth is a
Holy, holy, holy, Lord God of hosts.   Hebrew word.)

Benedictus qui venit in nomine Domini.
Blessed is he who cometh in the name of the Lord.

(5) OFFERTORIUM:

Domine Jesu Christe, Rex Gloriae, libera animas defunctorum de poenis inferni et de profundo lacu!
Lord Jesus Christ, King of Glory, free the souls of the departed from the punishment of Hell and from the deep pit!

(6) AGNUS DEI:

Agnus Dei, qui tollis peccata mundi, miserere nobis, dona nobis pacem!
Lamb of God, that takest away the sins of the world, have mercy upon us and grant us thy peace!

(7) LUX AETERNA:

Lux aeterna luceat eis!

Here are a few stanzas from the "Dies Irae", written by Thomas of Celano (c. AD 1190–1260), a Franciscan monk who was the first biographer of St Francis.

Dies irae, dies illa	*The day of wrath, that day*
Solvet saeclum in favilla,	*will dissolve the world in ashes,*
Teste David cum Sibylla.	*as David and the Sibyl have foretold.*
Quantus tremor est futurus,	*What fear and trembling there will be*
Quando iudex est venturus,	*when the judge will come*
Cuncta stricte discussurus.	*to examine everything strictly.*
Tuba mirum spargens sonum	*The trumpet, scattering its wondrous sound*
Per sepulcra regionum	*over the graves of all lands,*
Coget omnes ante thronum.	*will summon all souls before the throne.*
Mors stupebit et natura,	*Death and nature will be amazed*
Cum resurget creatura	*when all created things rise again*
Iudicanti responsura.	*to answer their judge.*
Liber scriptus proferetur,	*The written record will be brought out,*
In quo totum continetur	*in which everything is contained*
Unde mundus iudicetur.	*by which the world is to be judged.*

Later in the poem the writer speaks in the first person:

Quid sum miser tunc dicturus,	*What shall I, poor wretch that I am, say on that day?*
Quem patronum rogaturus,	*Whom shall I call upon as my advocate,*
Dum vix iustus sit securus?	*when even the righteous will scarcely escape unscathed?*
Recordare, Jesu pie,	*Remember, O merciful Jesus,*
Quod sum causa tuae viae,	*that I am the reason for your coming to earth!*
Ne me perdas illa die!	*Do not destroy me on that day!*

Confutatis maledictis,	*When the wicked have been condemned*
Flammis acribus addictis,	*and consigned to the fierce flames,*
Voca me cum benedictis!	*call me to be with the blessed ones!*

II. MEMORABLE SAYINGS

The sentiments expressed in the following memorable sayings are worthy of discussion:

1 *Decision and indecision*

    (a) Julius Caesar crosses the Rubicon and marches on Rome:

        iacta est alea. (Suetonius, *Julius* 32)

    (b) Hannibal fails to march on Rome after a crushing defeat on the Romans:

        vincere scis, Hannibal, victoria uti nescis. (Livy XXII.51)

2 *Some views of Roman conquest*

    (a) The destiny of Rome:
        tu regere imperio populos, Romane, memento
        (hae tibi erunt artes) pacisque imponere morem,
        parcere subiectis et debellare superbos.

        (Virgil, *Aeneid* VI.851)

    (b) A British chief's view:

        ubi solitudinem faciunt, pacem appellant. (Tacitus, *Agricola* 30)

    (c) The view of the imperious despot:

        oderint dum metuant. (Cicero, *Philippics* I.14)

    (d) A mad emperor's view:

        utinam populus Romanus unam cervicem haberet!

        (Suetonius, *Caligula* 30)

    (e) A pacifist view:

        cedant arma togae. (Cicero, *De Officiis* I.22)

3 *The glamour and tragedy of war:*

    (a) **dulce et decorum est pro patria mori.** (Horace, *Odes* III.ii.13)

    (b) **bella matribus detestata.** (Horace, *Odes* I.i.24)

4 *Death*

    (a) At the tomb of his brother:

        atque in perpetuum, frater, ave atque vale! (Catullus CI.10)

    (b) Death's even hand:

        pallida Mors aequo pulsat pede pauperum tabernas
        regumque turres. (Horace, *Odes* I.iv.13)

Hannibal

5 *The enduring power of the arts:*

    (a) The poet:

        exegi monumentum aere perennius.   (Horace, *Odes* III.xxx.1)

        non omnis moriar.   (Horace, *Odes* III.XXX.6)

    (b) The architect:

        si monumentum requiris, circumspice!   (Inscription on Christopher Wren's tomb in St Paul's Cathedral)

6 *Three mottoes for optimists:*

    (a) **forsan et haec olim meminisse iuvabit.**   (Virgil, *Aeneid* I.203)

    (b) **nil desperandum.**   (Horace, *Odes* I.vii.27)

    (c) **dum spiro, spero.**   (anon.)

7 *A clear conscience:*

    (a) **mens sibi conscia recti**   (Virgil, *Aeneid* I.604)

    (b) **integer vitae, scelerisque purus**   (Horace, *Odes* I.xxii.1)

8 *The ups and downs of love:*

    (a) **vivamus, mea Lesbia, atque amemus.**   (Catullus V.1)

    (b) **difficile est longum subito deponere amorem.**   (Catullus LVII.13)

    (c) **odi et amo: quare id faciam, fortasse, requiris.**
        nescio, sed fieri sentio et excrucior.   (Catullus LXXXV)

    (d) **varium et mutabile semper femina.**   (Virgil, *Aeneid* IV.569)

alea, -ae (*f*), die (singular of dice)
debello (1), to defeat
dum (+ *subj.*), provided that
cervix, -icis (*f*), neck
cedo (3) (+ *dat.*), to yield

decorus, -a, -um, noble
pallidus, -a, -um, pale
exigo (3), **-egi, -actum,** to complete, finish, perfect
integer (+ *gen.*), blameless (in)
excrucio (1), to torture

Miranda   THE STORY OF THE LATIN LANGUAGE 2

Classical Latin, as typified by such writers as Cicero, Caesar, Livy, Pliny, Catullus, Virgil, Ovid and Martial, is essentially a literary language. (See the Chronological Tables in *Ecce Romani* Book 5, pages 3 and 280–281.) As far as spoken Latin is concerned, the only clues we have are in the graffiti found in places like Pompeii and in occasional colloquialisms used in literature (e.g. in the plays of Plautus and Terence, and in the letters of Cicero).

Roman power began to be eclipsed in the fifth century AD. During the

Dark Ages which followed, literary Latin shrank to a trickle, apart from the writings of the Church; but Latin continued to be spoken in those areas which Rome had previously controlled. No language remains static; over the years, all languages evolve, and this is particularly true of spoken language. Gradually, therefore, different versions of Latin began to emerge in different parts of what had been the Roman empire, and it was not long before the various dialects became mutually unintelligible. These dialects continued to develop until they ultimately became languages in their own right, for example, Italian, French, Spanish, Portuguese and Rumanian. Although these Romance languages appear very different from one another, however, they can all be traced back to their Latin origins.

The first thing that began to disintegrate within Vulgar Latin (the term used to describe the language spoken during the period of flux) was the system of case-endings. "Vulgar" is derived from the Latin word **vulgus**, "common people". Nominative and Accusative were confused, and usually it was the Accusative form which survived. The functions of the other cases, which had already been usurped to some extent by prepositions even in the Classical language, began to be expressed entirely by prepositions. For example, the Genitive was expressed by **de**, meaning "of", the Dative by **ad**, meaning "to", and the Ablative by **de**, meaning "from". Some prepositions were actually joined together to produce more emphatic forms: for example, **ab** + **ante** ultimately became the French *avant* and the Italian *avanti;* and **de** + **ab** + **ante** became French *devant* and Italian *davanti.*

The pronouns **hic** and **is** virtually disappeared. On the other hand, **ille** vastly extended its territory, not only as the sole word for "he", "she", "it", "they", "him", "her" and "them", but also taking on a new lease of life as the definite article "the". For example, *il, elle, le, la, les* and *leur* in French, *el, la, los* and *las* in Spanish, are all derived from forms of *ille.*

For the learner of Latin (in ancient times, as today), perhaps the most intimidating feature is the vast array of tense formations and person endings. Person endings in the Romance languages still show their Latin origin, e.g.

English	Latin	Italian	French	Spanish	Portuguese	Rumanian
we sing	cantamus	cantiamo	chantons	cantamos	cantamos	cintam
you sang	cantavisti cantasti	cantasti	chantas	cantaste	cantaste	cintashi

In Classical Latin, the perfect tense has two basic meanings: e.g. **cantavi** can mean "I sang" or "I have sung". In Vulgar Latin (and even occasionally in Classical Latin), **habeo** + the past participle became the normal way to express the latter meaning; and this became the norm in most Romance languages, e.g.

English	Latin	French	Italian	Rumanian
I have sung	habeo cantatum	j'ai chanté	ho cantato	am cantat

Finally, since colloquial speech is the "homeland" of slang, slang expressions tended to oust more formal Latin words. For example, the French word for "horse" (*le cheval*) comes, not from **equus,** but from

caballus, "a nag". Compare *la tête* which is derived from **testa,** "a tile". Some words proved so difficult to learn that they disappeared without trace. The verb **loquor** is a notable example. The Church word **parabula** (meaning "parable") came to mean "word" in general, and related to it was the verb **parabulare,** "to speak". From this developed the Italian *parlare* and the French *parler* and *parole*. On the other hand, the Spanish and Portuguese verbs for "speak" (*hablar* and *falar* respectively) came from the colloquial word **fabulari,** which is quite common in Plautus.

You will have grasped that the study of the development of language is a vast and complex subject far beyond the scope of this book. It is hoped, however, that the above notes (which have attempted to give only a taste of some of the changes which have occurred) will have aroused your curiosity sufficiently to encourage you to delve more deeply into what can be a really fascinating subject.

Aenigma   **Politics and Law**

All the words in this crossword are connected with the political and legal organisation of Rome. (*The solution is on page 145.*)

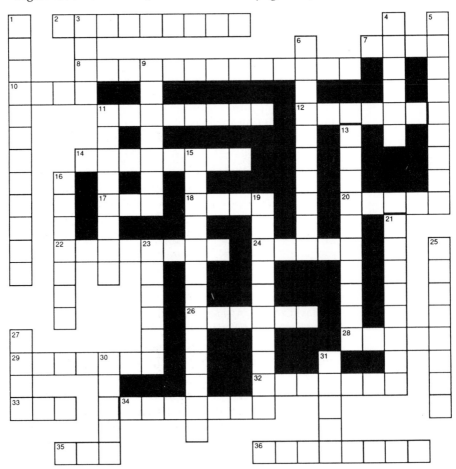

Across

2 Elderly statesmen. (9)
7 Being a "New" one was a matter of rejoicing for an up-and-coming politician. (4)
8 A ladder for ambitious politicians. (6, 7)
10 Term of contempt in court. (4)
11 A "bridge builder" between gods and men. (8)
12 Fatherland. (6)
14 An autocrat, but not necessarily a usurper of power in Rome. (8)
17 Abbreviated consuls appear like a small island. (3)
18 Rights. (4)
20 The hub of political and business activity in Rome. (5)
22 Supreme power. (8)
24 The meeting place of the Senate. (5)
26 Same people as 2 Across, although they do not sound as old. (6)
28 Cicero expresses outrage at the state of the world: **"o tempora! o _____".** (5)
29 Along with 33 Across describes the public weal and the state as a whole. (7)
32 They supervised the city services. (7)
33 See 29 Across. (3)
34 Businessmen on horseback? (7)
35 Law. (3)
36 These two men counted a lot, but only every five years. (8)

Down

1 "without trial" (7, 5)
3 A "pointing" word which should be very familiar to our readers. (4)
4 Assembly of the people. (6)
5 Along with 9 Down describes a decision of the Senate. (7, 9)
6 Provincial governor of the second rank. (10)
9 See 5 Down.
11 Imperial title. (8)
13 The right to vote. (10)
15 Representatives of the common people. (7, 6)
16 Elections. (7)
19 Power based on personal influence. (10)
21 Though deprived of their "chopping" weapon, their rods still showed the consuls' power. (8)
23 Raised platform in the Forum. (6)
25 Finance was his business. (8)
27 These four letters represented the Senate and People of Rome. (4)
30 A member of the jury. (5)
31 The ultimate rulers of Rome, at least theoretically. (5)

Appendix I

(a) Abbreviations from Latin

Abbreviation	Latin	Meaning
ab init.	ab initio	from the beginning
AD	anno Domini	in the year of the Lord
ad fin.	ad finem	at (towards) the end
ad init.	ad initium	at the beginning
ad lib.	ad libitum	at pleasure
a.m.	ante meridiem	before midday
cf.	confer	compare
circ. ⎤ c. ⎦	circa, circum, circiter	about
con.	contra	against
CV	curriculum vitae	outline of one's career
DG	Dei gratia	by the grace of God
DV	Deo volente	God willing
e.g.	exempli gratia	for example
et al.	et alii (alia)	and others
etc.	et cetera	and the rest, and so on
et seq.	et sequentes	and the following
ex div.	extra dividendum	without dividend, dividend payable to seller
F.D. ⎤ Fid. Def. ⎦	Fidei Defensor	Defender of the Faith
fl.	floruit	period when a celebrity flourished
ib. ⎤ ibid. ⎦	ibidem	in the same book (chapter)
i.e.	id est	that is
inf.	infra	below, further on in the passage
infra dig.	infra dignitatem	beneath one's dignity
inst.	instanti mense	in the present month
loc. cit.	loco citato	in the passage just quoted
MS	manu scriptum	manuscript
NB	nota bene	note well
nem. con.	nemine contradicente	no one speaking against
no.	numero	number
ob.	obiit	(date when someone) died
op. cit.	opere citato	in the work just quoted
per pro. ⎤ pp. ⎦	per procurationem	through the agency of, for and on behalf of
p.m.	post meridiem	after midday
PPS	post postscriptum	additional postscript
PS	postscriptum	something written afterwards
pro tem.	pro tempore	for the time being
prox.	proximo (mense)	next month
Q.E.D.	quod erat demonstrandum	which was to be proved
q.v.	quod vide!	Look it up! (lit. "which see")
R.	rex, regina	king, queen
R.I.P.	Requiescat in Pace	may he (she) rest in peace
sc.	scilicet	namely (supplying a missing word)

Abbreviation	Latin	Meaning
sq.	sequens	following
sqq.	sequentes	(more than one thing) following
sub fin.	sub fine	near the end
s.v.	sub voce (verbo)	(look it up) under that heading (or word)
ult.	ultimo (mense)	last month
v. vid. }	vide	see! look up! consult!
viz.	videlicet	namely
v. vs }	versus	against

(b) Abbreviations in Latin

The Romans also had their abbreviated forms. For example, when writing, they usually shortened all the forenames (P. for Publius, M. for Marcus, etc.), the names of months (Feb.; Mart.; Oct.) and the special days in the month (Kal.; Non.; Id.). Inscriptions also have a large vocabulary of abbreviations (see page 56).

a.d.	ante diem	(used in calculating dates)
A.U.C.	ab urbe condita	(counting) from the founding of Rome
cos. coss.	consule consulibus }	in the consulship of
SPQR	Senatus Populusque Romanus	the senate and people of Rome

Appendix II

Latin in Everyday Use

Latin phrases abound in legal language, and many of these are now commonly found in everyday language. Amongst the most common are the following:

alias ("at another time"): an assumed name

alibi ("elsewhere"): a claim to have been elsewhere at the time of the offence

a priori ("from the preceding"): arguing from known facts or assumptions to their effects (i.e. reasoning deductively)

bona fide ("in good faith"): genuine

caret: there is something missing (marked^)

caveat ("let him beware"): a notice giving a warning

caveat emptor ("let the buyer beware!"): denial of the seller's responsibility for the quality of merchandise

compos mentis ("in control of one's mind"): of sound mind

corpus delicti ("the body of the crime"): body of facts which prove a crime has taken place

de facto ("from the deed"): existing in fact, whether legally recognised or not

de iure ("in accordance with law"): by right, legally recognised

dies non: a day on which no business is transacted

ergo: therefore (introducing a conclusion)

ex gratia ("out of kindness"): with no acceptance of liability

ex parte: from one side only

flagrante delicto ("while the crime is still blazing"): in the act (of committing a crime)

habeas corpus ("produce the body"): writ ordering jailor to produce a prisoner in court and to state why he has been detained

in camera ("in a vaulted room"): in the judge's private room, i.e. in secret

in perpetuum: for ever

ipso facto: by that very act; thereby

modus operandi (often contracted to **MO**): method of working

mutatis mutandis ("the things which have to be changed having been changed"): with the necessary changes

obiter dictum: a passing remark, an "aside"

pari passu ("with equal step"): together, at an equal rate of progress/ development

per se ("through itself"): essentially, intrinsically

persona (non) grata: an (un)acceptable person (used especially of (dis)credited diplomats)

post hoc, ergo propter hoc ("after this, therefore because of this"): false reasoning (arguing that one thing caused another because it happened first)

prima facie: at first sight

pro bono publico: for the public good

pro forma: done in a set form, standard lay-out

pro rata: in proportion

quid pro quo ("what for what"): something (given in return) for something else

quorum ("of whom"): minimum number required to be present to conduct business

rigor mortis: stiffening of body after death

sic ("thus", "so"): often put in brackets after a word or remark that looks like a misprint or misspelling to assure the reader that the word/remark is exactly as the author wrote/spoke it

seriatim: in order, one after another

sine die ("without a (stipulated) day"): indefinitely

sine qua non ("without which not"): an indispensable condition

status quo: the existing state of affairs

status quo ante: the state of affairs that existed previously

stet ("let it stand"): i.e., ignore the correction

sub judice: under (judicial) consideration

sub poena ("under punishment"): writ ordering person to appear before a court or suffer a penalty

sub rosa ("under the rose"): secretly (in olden times, the rose was a symbol of secrecy)

supra: above, further back in the passage

ultra vires: beyond one's authority

verbatim: word for word

vice versa ("the order having been reversed"): the other way round

Fabricanda

Catapulta

This catapult is designed to fire solid objects.
A javelin-firing catapult would require a narrower groove (A).

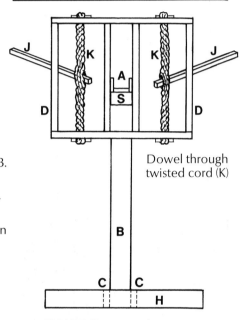

Dowel through twisted cord (K)

Arms (J) not shown

Hinge

The trajectory is adjusted by moving F into positions 1, 2 or 3

T is a metal plate. The bottom is screwed to B. Through the top there is a bolt which passes through S to another T on other side. Ensure that the space between S and B is big enough to let S pivot when trajectory is adjusted.

SIDE VIEW

Dowel through twisted cord (K)

FRONT VIEW

Twisted cord (K) comes up through hole drilled in D. The dowel is used to twist the cord so that arms (J) spring back into position shown by dotted line.

The arms (J) should be level with the top of A.

Groove for projectile
The back end is made solid by inserting block X. At the front, the sides are fixed to the inner uprights of frame D.

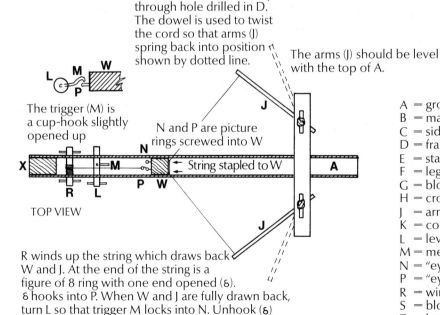

The trigger (M) is a cup-hook slightly opened up

N and P are picture rings screwed into W

String stapled to W

TOP VIEW

R winds up the string which draws back W and J. At the end of the string is a figure of 8 ring with one end opened (ᛞ). ᛞ hooks into P. When W and J are fully drawn back, turn L so that trigger M locks into N. Unhook (ᛞ) The catapult is fired by turning L to release M.

A = groove for projectile
B = main support pillar
C = sides of base
D = frame for "spring"
E = stay to support pillar B
F = leg to adjust the trajectory
G = block in base to which E is fixed
H = cross supports to keep catapult erect
J = arms of "spring"
K = cord/rope twisted to create "spring"
L = lever to release trigger
M = metal trigger
N = "eye" into which trigger fits
P = "eye" on W used to crank back J/W
R = winch to crank back J/W
S = block under A to which T is fixed
T = bracket on which top of catapult pivots
W = block to which firing string is fixed
X = block used to firm up end of groove (A)

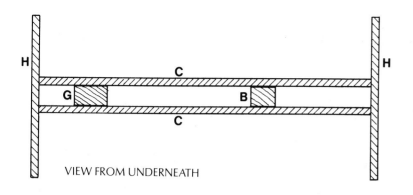

VIEW FROM UNDERNEATH

103

Onager

Used to hurl boulders at enemy walls

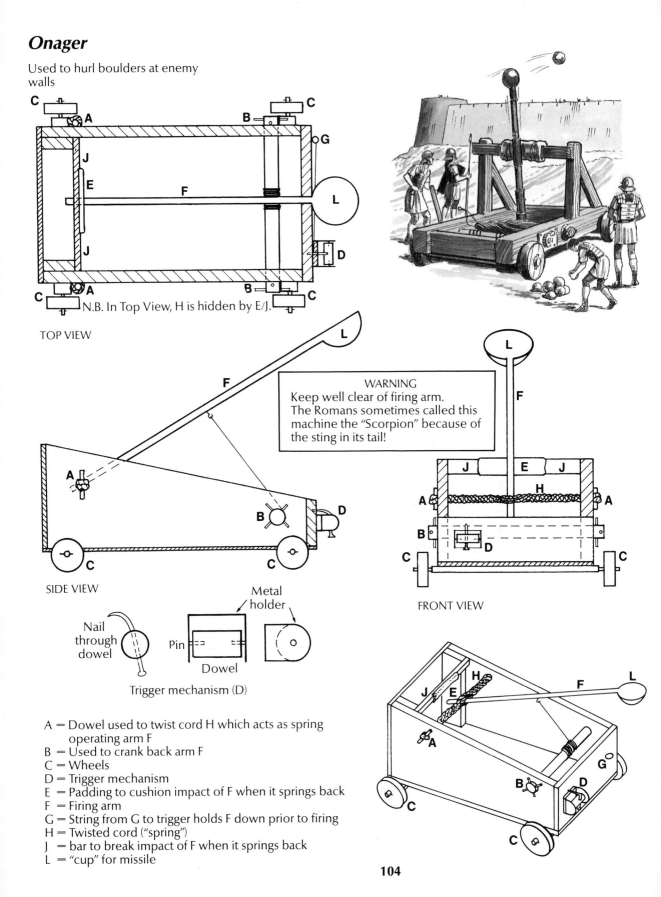

N.B. In Top View, H is hidden by E/J.

TOP VIEW

WARNING
Keep well clear of firing arm.
The Romans sometimes called this
machine the "Scorpion" because of
the sting in its tail!

SIDE VIEW

FRONT VIEW

Nail through dowel

Metal holder

Pin

Dowel

Trigger mechanism (D)

A = Dowel used to twist cord H which acts as spring
    operating arm F
B = Used to crank back arm F
C = Wheels
D = Trigger mechanism
E = Padding to cushion impact of F when it springs back
F = Firing arm
G = String from G to trigger holds F down prior to firing
H = Twisted cord ("spring")
J = bar to break impact of F when it springs back
L = "cup" for missile

104

Aries and Vinea

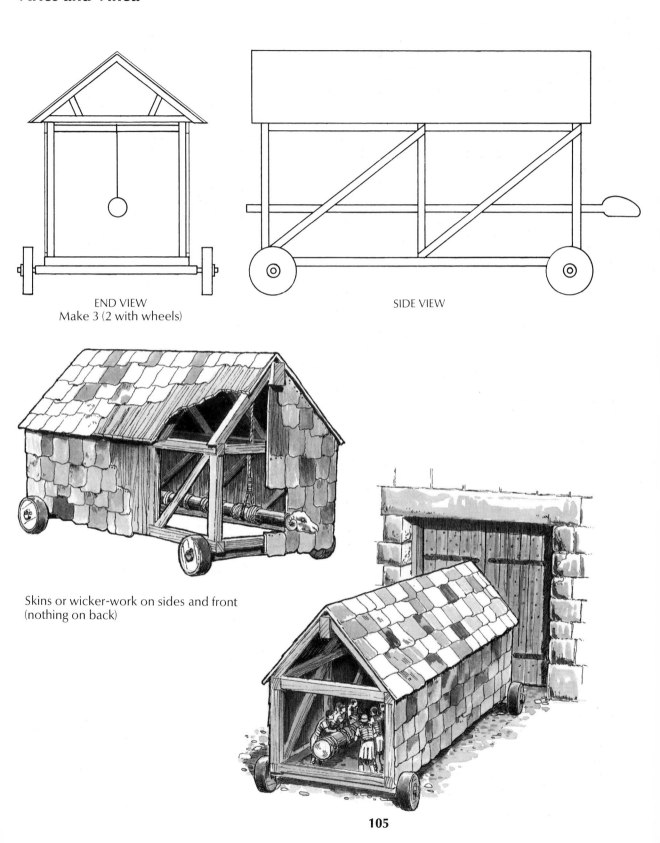

END VIEW
Make 3 (2 with wheels)

SIDE VIEW

Skins or wicker-work on sides and front
(nothing on back)

Tables

Section A: Nouns

		Group 1	Group 2			Group 3			Group 4		Group 5
Sing.	Nom.	puella	servus	puer	baculum	vox	civis	nomen	manus	cornu	dies
	Acc.	puellam	servum	puerum	baculum	vocem	civem	nomen	manum	cornu	diem
	Gen.	puellae	servi	pueri	baculi	vocis	civis	nominis	manus	cornus	diei
	Dat.	puellae	servo	puero	baculo	voci	civi	nomini	manui	cornu	diei
	Abl.	puella	servo	puero	baculo	voce	cive	nomine	manu	cornu	die
Plur.	Nom.	puellae	servi	pueri	bacula	voces	cives	nomina	manus	cornua	dies
	Acc.	puellas	servos	pueros	bacula	voces	cives	nomina	manus	cornua	dies
	Gen.	puellarum	servorum	puerorum	baculorum	vocum	civium	nominum	manuum	cornuum	dierum
	Dat.	puellis	servis	pueris	baculis	vocibus	civibus	nominibus	manibus	cornibus	diebus
	Abl.	puellis	servis	pueris	baculis	vocibus	civibus	nominibus	manibus	cornibus	diebus

1 *Vocative Case.* This case is used when someone or something is addressed by name. It is only in the singular of Group 2 nouns ending in **-us** that it has a different ending from the nominative case, e.g. **amice, Marce, Corneli, Gai.**

2 The *stem* of a noun is that part which remains when the genitive singular ending is removed, e.g. **puella**, genitive singular **puellae**, stem **puell-; vox, vocis,** stem **voc-; nomen, nominis,** stem **nomin-.**

3 In Group 3 nouns, there is no standard form for the nominative singular (e.g. **mater, vestis, urbs,** etc.); and there are two forms of the genitive plural (**-um** and **-ium**).

4 **domus** usually has the same endings as **manus.** Common exceptions are ablative singular (**domo**) and the special form **domi,** *at home.*

5 *Gender:*

(a) Group 1 nouns are all feminine except those which are men's names, jobs that men did, or the names of certain rivers, e.g. **Caligula, -ae** (*m*); **nauta, -ae** (*m*), sailor; **Matrona, -ae** (*m*), Marne.

(b) Group 2 nouns ending in **-us** or **-er** are nearly all masculine, but names of cities, islands and trees are feminine, e.g. **Corinthus, -i** (*f*), Corinth; **laurus, -i** (*f*), bay-tree. Group 2 nouns ending in **-um** are neuter.

(c) Most nouns in Group 3 are either masculine or feminine, but nearly all nouns of the following types are neuter:
ending in **-en,** **-inis** : e.g. **nomen, nominis** (*n*)
ending in **-us,** **-oris** : e.g. **corpus, corporis** (*n*)
ending in **-us, -eris** : e.g. **onus, oneris** (*n*)

(d) Group 4 nouns ending in **-us** are mostly masculine, but two common exceptions are **manus, -us** (*f*) and **domus, -us** (*f*).

(e) Group 5 nouns are all feminine except **dies, diei** (*m*) and **meridies, -ei** (*m*). When **dies** refers to a fixed day it is feminine, e.g. **die constituta,** *on the appointed day.*

Section B: Adjectives

		Group 1/2			Group 3			
		Masc.	Fem.	Neut.	Masc./Fem.	Neut.	Masc./Fem.	Neut.
Sing.	Nom.	magnus	magna	magnum	omnis	omne	ingens	ingens
	Acc.	magnum	magnam	magnum	omnem	omne	ingentem	ingens
	Gen.	magni	magnae	magni	omnis	omnis	ingentis	ingentis
	Dat.	magno	magnae	magno	omni	omni	ingenti	ingenti
	Abl.	magno	magna	magno	omni	omni	ingenti	ingenti
Plur.	Nom.	magni	magnae	magna	omnes	omnia	ingentes	ingentia
	Acc.	magnos	magnas	magna	omnes	omnia	ingentes	ingentia
	Gen.	magnorum	magnarum	magnorum	omnium	omnium	ingentium	ingentium
	Dat.	magnis	magnis	magnis	omnibus	omnibus	ingentibus	ingentibus
	Abl.	magnis	magnis	magnis	omnibus	omnibus	ingentibus	ingentibus

1 In general, nouns and adjectives of the same group have the same case endings. Thus,

magnus has the same endings as **servus**
magna has the same endings as **puella**
magnum has the same endings as **baculum**.

However, in Group 3, whereas most nouns have their ablative singular ending in **-e**, most adjectives have their ablative singular ending in **-i**. Exceptions are **dives, -itis** (*rich*), **pauper, -eris** (*poor*), **vetus, -eris** (*old*) and comparative adjectives, all of which have their ablative singular ending in **-e**.

2 Some adjectives of Groups 1/2 end in **-er** in the nominative singular masculine, e.g.

noster, nostra, nostrum
miser, misera, miserum

The endings of the other cases are the same as for **magnus, -a, -um.**

3 There is no standard form for the nominative singular endings of Group 3 adjectives.

4 Some common adjectives of Groups 1/2 have the genitive singular ending in **-ius** and the dative singular ending in **-i; solus** (*alone*), **totus** (*all*), **ullus** (*any*), **nullus** (*none*), **uter** (*which*), **neuter** (*neither*), **alter** (*the other*).

5 Adjectives are sometimes used as nouns, e.g. **nostri** (*our men*), **boni** (*good people*), **bona** (*goods*).

Section C: Comparison of Adjectives

1 Adjectives have Positive, Comparative and Superlative forms. The Comparative can usually be recognised by the ending **-ior**. The Superlative can usually be recognised by the endings **-issimus**, **-errimus** or **-illimus**, e.g.

Positive	*Comparative*	*Superlative*
ignavus	**ignavior**	**ignavissimus**
felix	**felicior**	**felicissimus**
pulcher	**pulchrior**	**pulcherrimus**
facilis	**facilior**	**facillimus**

2 Comparative adjectives have the same endings as **melior** in the table opposite. The Comparative has several possible meanings, e.g. **ignavior** may mean *lazier, more lazy, rather lazy, too lazy.*

3 Superlative adjectives have the same endings as **magnus, -a, -um**. The Superlative also has several possible meanings, e.g. **ignavissimus** may mean *laziest, most lazy, very lazy, exceedingly lazy.*

4 Some adjectives have irregular Comparative and Superlative forms, e.g.

bonus, good	**melior,** better	**optimus,** best
malus, bad	**peior,** worse	**pessimus,** worst
magnus, big	**maior,** bigger	**maximus,** biggest
parvus, small	**minor,** smaller	**minimus,** smallest
multus, much	**plus,** more	**plurimus,** most
multi, many	**plures,** more	**plurimi,** most

5 The Comparative Adjective forms:

	Singular		Plural	
	M./F.	N.	M./F.	N.
Nom.	melior	melius	meliores	meliora
Acc.	meliorem	melius	meliores	meliora
Gen.	melioris		meliorum	meliorum
Dat.	meliori		melioribus	melioribus
Abl.	meliore		melioribus	melioribus

108

Section D: Adverbs

Adverbs are of various types. Two of the most common types are:

1 Adverbs derived from adjectives. There are three common endings:

(a) **-e**, e.g. **longe** (from longus), **maxime** (from maximus)
(b) **-o**, e.g. **subito** (from subitus), **tuto** (from tutus)
(c) **-iter** or **-ter**, e.g. **fortiter** (from fortis), **audacter** (from audax)

2 Adverbs based on prepositions, e.g.:

postea (from **post ea**). Compare **antea, praeterea, propterea, interea** (based on the prepositions **ante, praeter, propter, inter**).

Section E: Comparison of Adverbs

Adverbs have Positive, Comparative and Superlative forms.

1 The Comparative can be recognised by the ending **-ius**. The Superlative can be recognised by the endings **-issime**, **-errime** or **-illime**, e.g.:

Positive	Comparative	Superlative
ignave	ignavius	ignavissime
feliciter	felicius	felicissime
pulchre	pulchrius	pulcherrime
facile	facilius	facillime

2 Some adverbs have irregular Comparative and Superlative forms (compare the corresponding adjectives on page 108), e.g.:

bene, well	**melius**, better	**optime**, best
male, badly	**peius**, worse	**pessime**, worst
magnopere, greatly	**magis**, more	**maxime**, most
paulum, a little	**minus**, less	**minime**, least
multum, much	**plus**, more	**plurimum**, most

3 The Comparative adverb, like the corresponding adjective, has several possible meanings, e.g. **ignavius** may mean *more lazily, rather lazily, too lazily.*

4 The Superlative adverb also has several possible meanings, e.g. **ignavissime** can mean *most lazily, very lazily, in an extremely lazy way.*

Section F: A Special Use of *quam* + Superlative

quam + a Superlative adjective or adverb has a special meaning, e.g.:
quam plurimi, *as many as possible*
quam celerrime, *as quickly as possible*
milites quam plurimos duxit, *he brought as many soldiers as he could.*

Section G: Demonstrative Adjectives

		Masc.	Fem.	Neut.	Masc.	Fem.	Neut.	Masc.	Fem.	Neut.
Sing.	Nom.	hic	haec	hoc	ille	illa	illud	is	ea	id
	Acc.	hunc	hanc	hoc	illum	illam	illud	eum	eam	id
	Gen.	huius	huius	huius	illius	illius	illius	eius	eius	eius
	Dat.	huic	huic	huic	illi	illi	illi	ei	ei	ei
	Abl.	hoc	hac	hoc	illo	illa	illo	eo	ea	eo
Plur.	Nom.	hi	hae	haec	illi	illae	illa	ei	eae	ea
	Acc.	hos	has	haec	illos	illas	illa	eos	eas	ea
	Gen.	horum	harum	horum	illorum	illarum	illorum	eorum	earum	eorum
	Dat.	his	his	his	illis	illis	illis	eis	eis	eis
	Abl.	his	his	his	illis	illis	illis	eis	eis	eis

Notes:

1 **haec** mulier cum **eis** pueris ambulabat. **This** *woman was walking with* **those** *boys.*
ille senator risit. **That** *senator laughed.*
eam puellam vidimus. *We saw* **that** *girl.*

2 The above Demonstrative Adjectives are also used as 3rd person pronouns, e.g.:

haec cum **eis** ambulabat. **She** *was walking with* **them.**
ille risit. **He** *laughed.*
eam vidimus. *We saw* **her.**

3 The genitive forms may be used to indicate possession, e.g.:

patrem **eius** vidimus. *We saw* **his/her** *father.*
amicos **illorum** servavi. *I saved* **their** *friends.*

(See also Note 3 on page 112.)

4 The adjective **iste, ista, istud** (*that of yours*) has the same endings as **ille**. It can also be used as a pronoun, most often in court cases, speaking contemptuously of "the accused".

110

		Masc.	Fem.	Neut.		Masc.	Fem.	Neut.
Sing.	Nom.	idem	eadem	idem		ipse	ipsa	ipsum
	Acc.	eundem	eandem	idem		ipsum	ipsam	ipsum
	Gen.	eiusdem	eiusdem	eiusdem		ipsius	ipsius	ipsius
	Dat.	eidem	eidem	eidem		ipsi	ipsi	ipsi
	Abl.	eodem	eadem	eodem		ipso	ipsa	ipso
Plur.	Nom.	eidem	eaedem	eadem		ipsi	ipsae	ipsa
	Acc.	eosdem	easdem	eadem		ipsos	ipsas	ipsa
	Gen.	eorundem	earundem	eorundem		ipsorum	ipsarum	ipsorum
	Dat.	eisdem	eisdem	eisdem		ipsis	ipsis	ipsis
	Abl.	eisdem	eisdem	eisdem		ipsis	ipsis	ipsis

Notes:

1 **idem, eadem, idem**, *the same*, has the same forms as **is, ea, id** with the addition of **-dem**. Note that **-m-** is changed to **-n-** in the accusative singular (masc. and fem.) and in the genitive plural; and the nominative and accusative singular neuter is **idem**.

2 **ipse, ipsa, ipsum** is used to give emphasis to a noun or pronoun, e.g.:

ego **ipse** veni, *I myself came.*

ipse venit, *He came himself.*

Caesarem **ipsum** vidimus, *We saw Caesar himself.*

aedificia **ipsa** vidimus, *We saw the actual buildings.*

      the very buildings.

      the buildings themselves.

Section H: Interrogative, Relative and Indefinite Pronouns

		Interrogative Pronoun (who? what?)			Relative Pronoun (who, which, that)			Indefinite Pronoun (a certain)		
		Masc.	Fem.	Neut.	Masc.	Fem.	Neut.	Masc.	Fem.	Neut.
Sing.	Nom.	quis?	quis?	quid?	qui	quae	quod	quidam	quaedam	quoddam
	Acc.	quem?	quem?	quid?	quem	quam	quod	quendam	quandam	quoddam
	Gen.	cuius?	cuius?	cuius?	cuius	cuius	cuius	cuiusdam	cuiusdam	cuiusdam
	Dat.	cui?	cui?	cui?	cui	cui	cui	cuidam	cuidam	cuidam
	Abl.	quo?	qua?	quo?	quo	qua	quo	quodam	quadam	quodam
Plur.	Nom.	qui?	quae?	quae?	qui	quae	quae	quidam	quaedam	quaedam
	Acc.	quos?	quas?	quae?	quos	quas	quae	quosdam	quasdam	quaedam
	Gen.	quorum?	quarum?	quorum?	quorum	quarum	quorum	quorundam	quarundam	quorundam
	Dat.	quibus?	quibus?	quibus?	quibus	quibus	quibus	quibusdam	quibusdam	quibusdam
	Abl.	quibus?	quibus?	quibus?	quibus	quibus	quibus	quibusdam	quibusdam	quibusdam

Notes:

1 The Interrogative and Relative Pronouns have the same forms, except in the nominative and accusative singular.

2 The Interrogative Adjectives has the same forms as the Relative Pronoun, e.g. **quod** templum visitavisti? **Which** *temple did you visit?*

3 **quidam, quaedam, quoddam** (*a certain*) is a compound of the Relative Pronoun and the ending **-dam**. It has the same forms as the Relative Pronoun, except that **-m-** changes to **-n-** before **-d-**. (Cf. **idem**.)   **quidam** is used both as a pronoun and as an adjective, e.g.:
  quidam advenit, **A certain man** *has arrived.*
  homines **quosdam** vidimus, *We saw* **some men.**

4 **aliquis, aliquis, aliquid** is the usual word for *someone/something*, e.g.:
  aliquem misit.   *He sent someone.*
  aliquid vini bibimus.   *We drank some wine.*

  aliquis has the same forms as **quis, quis, quid.**

5 Words for *anyone/anything* include
  (a) **quisquam, quidquam** (or **quicquam**) which is used after negatives or **vix** (*scarcely, hardly*), e.g.:
    vix quisquam venit.   *Scarcely anyone came.*
    nec quidquam apparuit.   *And nothing appeared.*

    The forms are the same as for **quis, quis, quid** followed by the suffix **-quam.**

  (b) **quis, quis, quid**, which is used after **si, nisi, ne, num, quo, quanto**, e.g.:
    si quis te viderit, . . . *If anyone sees you,* . . . .

6 **quisquis, quidquid** means *whoever/whatever*. It has the same forms as **quis, quis, quid** (see page 113) in both parts, e.g.:
  quoquo modo   *in whatever way*

  In the neuter, both **quidquid** and **quicquid** are found in the nominative and accusative.

7 **quicunque, quaecunque, quodcunque** means *whoever/whatever*. It is a compound of the relative **qui, quae, quod** (see page 113) and the ending **-cunque**, e.g.:
  quacunque de re   *for whatever reason*

Section I: Personal Pronouns and Possessive Adjectives

		Personal Pronouns		Possessive Adjectives	
		1st Person	2nd Person	1st Person	2nd Person
Sing.	Nom. Acc. Gen. Dat. Abl.	ego me mei mihi me	tu te tui tibi te	meus, -a, -um	tuus, -a, -um
Plur.	Nom. Acc. Gen. Dat. Abl.	nos nos nostrum } nostri } nobis nobis	vos vos vestrum } vestri } vobis vobis	noster, nostra, nostrum	vester, vestra, vestrum

Notes:

1 The personal pronouns are used as Reflexive Pronouns in the 1st and 2nd persons, e.g.: **me** servavi, *I saved* **myself**.
nos liberavimus, *We set* **ourselves** *free*.

2 A special Reflexive pronoun is used for the 3rd person (singular and plural) meaning *himself, herself, itself, themselves:*

			Possessive Adjective
Acc.	se		suus, -a, -um,
Gen.	sui		*his, her, its, their own*
Dat.	sibi		
Abl.	se		

3 The preposition **cum** is used *after* Personal, Reflexive and Relative Pronouns, e.g. **mecum**, *with me*; **nobiscum**, *with us*; **secum**, *with himself*; **quibuscum**, *with whom*.

114

Section J: Numerals

Cardinal numerals are the numbers used in counting: "one," "two," "three," etc.

Ordinal numerals give the order in a series: "first," "second," "third," etc.

		Cardinals	*Ordinals*
1	I	unus, -a, -um	primus
2	II	duo, duae, duo	secundus
3	III	tres, tres, tria	tertius
4	IV	quattuor	quartus
5	V	quinque	quintus
6	VI	sex	sextus
7	VII	septem	septimus
8	VIII	octo	octavus
9	IX	novem	nonus
10	X	decem	decimus
11	XI	undecim	undecimus
12	XII	duodecim	duodecimus
13	XIII	tredecim	tertius decimus
14	XIV	quattuordecim	quartus decimus
15	XV	quindecim	quintus decimus
16	XVI	sedecim	sextus decimus
17	XVII	septendecim	septimus decimus
18	XVIII	duodeviginti	duodevicesimus
19	XIX	undeviginti	undevicesimus
20	XX	viginti	vicesimus
21	XXI	viginti unus	vicesimus primus
22	XXII	viginti duo	vicesimus secundus
23	XXIII	viginti tres	vicesimus tertius

		Cardinals	*Ordinals*
30	XXX	triginta	tricesimus
40	XL	quadraginta	quadragesimus
50	L	quinquaginta	quinquagesimus
60	LX	sexaginta	sexagesimus
70	LXX	septuaginta	septuagesimus
80	LXXX	octoginta	octogesimus
90	XC	nonaginta	nonagesimus
100	C	centum	centesimus
101	CI	centum et unus	centesimus primus
120	CXX	centum et viginti	centesimus vicesimus
200	CC	ducenti, -ae, -a	ducentesimus
300	CCC	trecenti, -ae, -a	trecentesimus
400	CCCC	quadringenti, -ae, -a	quadringentesimus
500	D	quingenti, -ae, -a	quingentesimus
600	DC	sescenti, -ae, -a	sescentesimus
700	DCC	septingenti, -ae, -a	septingentesimus
800	DCCC	octingenti, -ae, -a	octingentesimus
900	DCCCC	nongenti, -ae, -a	nongentesimus
1000	M	mille	millesimus
2000	MM	duo milia	bis millesimus

	M.	F.	N.	M.	F.	N.	M./F.	N.
Nom.	unus	una	unum	duo	duae	duo	tres	tria
Acc.	unum	unam	unum	duos	duas	duo	tres	tria
Gen.	unius	unius	unius	duorum	duarum	duorum	trium	trium
Dat.	uni	uni	uni	duobus	duabus	duobus	tribus	tribus
Abl.	uno	una	uno	duobus	duabus	duobus	tribus	tribus

N.B. The genitive and dative endings of **unus** are like **solus, totus**, etc. (See page 107.)

Notes:

(a) Of the cardinals, only the following decline (i.e. change their endings): **unus, duo, tres; ducenti** to **nongenti**; and **milia** (the plural of **mille**).

(b) The "hundreds" (**ducenti** to **nongenti**) are declined like the plural of **magnus, -a, -um.**

(c) **milia** is a plural noun of Group 3 and is generally followed by the genitive case, e.g. **tria milia servorum**, *3000 slaves*.

(d) All the ordinals are declined like **magnus, -a, -um.**

Section K: Verbs

(a) *Principal Parts*

When we refer to Latin verbs, we normally give four principal parts, e.g.:

	Present	Present Infinitive	Perfect Active	Supine	Meaning
Group 1	porto	portare (1)	portavi	portatum	*to carry*
Group 2	habeo	habere (2)	habui	habitum	*to have*
Group 3	mitto	mittere (3)	misi	missum	*to send*
Group 4	audio	audire (4)	audivi	auditum	*to hear*

Most verbs in Groups 1, 2 and 4 follow the above patterns. There is no standard form for the verbs in Group 3. This section will help you if you know which verb you are dealing with but are in some doubt about the form used.

All parts of the verb can be identified from the four principal parts. The following table of the verb **portare** illustrates this:

Principal Parts	**porto, portare** (1) Present stem: **porta-**			**portavi** Perfect stem: **portav-**		**portatum** Supine stem: **portat-**		
		Active	*Passive*		*Active*		*Active*	*Passive*
Indicative	Present Imperf. Future	porto portabam portabo	portor portabar portabor	Perfect Pluperf. Fut. Perf.	portavi portaveram portavero	Perfect Pluperf. Fut. Perf.	— — —	portatus sum portatus eram portatus ero
Subjunctive	Present Imperf.	portem portarem	porter portarer	Perfect Pluperf.	portaverim portavissem	Perfect Pluperf.	—	portatus sim portatus essem
Infinitive	Present	portare	portari	Perfect	portavisse	Perfect Future	— portaturus esse	portatus esse portatum iri
Participle	Present	portans	—	—	—	Perfect Future	— portaturus	portatus —
Imperative	Present	porta portate	portare portamini	—	—		—	—

116

(b) *Person Endings*

		Active		Passive	
		All tenses except Perfect	Perfect	Present Imperfect Future	Perfect Pluperfect Future Perf.
Sing.	1 2 3	**-o, -m** **-s** **-t**	**-i** **-isti** **-it**	**-r** **-ris** **-tur**	See Note (c).
Plur.	1 2 3	**-mus** **-tis** **-nt**	**-imus** **-istis** **-erunt**	**-mur** **-mini** **-ntur**	

(c) *Agreement of Subject and Verb*

In the Perfect, Pluperfect and Future Perfect tenses Passive,
the perfect participle passive (**-us, -a, -um**) agrees with the
subject of the verb in gender, number and case, e.g.:

puer laudat**us** est.	*The boy has been (was) praised.*
matres laudat**ae** sunt.	*The mothers have been (were) praised.*
aedificium laudat**um** est.	*The building has been (was) praised.*

(d) *Meanings of Tenses*

Tense	Active	Passive
Present	**portat,** *he carries, is carrying*	**portatur,** *he is carried, is being carried*
Imperfect	**portabat,** *he carried* *he kept on carrying* *he was carrying* *he used to carry* *he began to carry* *he tried to carry*	**portabatur,** *he was carried* *he was being carried* *he used to be carried*
Future	**portabit,** *he will carry*	**portabitur,** *he will be carried*
Perfect	**portavit,** *he carried* *he has carried*	**portatus est,** *he was carried* *he has been carried*
Pluperfect	**portaverat,** *he had carried*	**portatus erat,** *he had been carried*
Future Perfect	**portaverit,** *he will have carried*	**portatus erit,** *he will have been carried*

ACTIVE

Indicative

Group	Present	Imperfect	Future	Perfect	Pluperfect	Future Perfect
1	port**o** porta**s** porta**t** porta**mus** porta**tis** porta**nt**	porta**bam** porta**bas** porta**bat** porta**bamus** porta**batis** porta**bant**	porta**bo** porta**bis** porta**bit** porta**bimus** porta**bitis** porta**bunt**	portavi portav**isti** portav**it** portav**imus** portav**istis** portav**erunt**	portav**eram** portav**eras** portav**erat** portav**eramus** portav**eratis** portav**erant**	portav**ero** portav**eris** portav**erit** portav**erimus** portav**eritis** portav**erint**
2	habe**o** habe**s** habe**t** habe**mus** habe**tis** habe**nt**	habe**bam** habe**bas** habe**bat** habe**bamus** habe**batis** habe**bant**	habe**bo** habe**bis** habe**bit** habe**bimus** habe**bitis** habe**bunt**	habui habu**isti** habu**it** habu**imus** habu**istis** habu**erunt**	habu**eram** habu**eras** habu**erat** habu**eramus** habu**eratis** habu**erant**	habu**ero** habu**eris** habu**erit** habu**erimus** habu**eritis** habu**erint**
3	mitt**o** mitt**is** mitt**it** mitt**imus** mitt**itis** mitt**unt**	mitte**bam** mitte**bas** mitte**bat** mitte**bamus** mitte**batis** mitte**bant**	mitt**am** mitt**es** mitt**et** mitt**emus** mitt**etis** mitt**ent**	misi mis**isti** mis**it** mis**imus** mis**istis** mis**erunt**	mis**eram** mis**eras** mis**erat** mis**eramus** mis**eratis** mis**erant**	mis**ero** mis**eris** mis**erit** mis**erimus** mis**eritis** mis**erint**
	capi**o** capi**s** capi**t** capi**mus** capi**tis** capi**unt**	capie**bam** capie**bas** capie**bat** capie**bamus** capie**batis** capie**bant**	capi**am** capi**es** capi**et** capi**emus** capi**etis** capi**ent**	cepi cep**isti** cep**it** cep**imus** cep**istis** cep**erunt**	cep**eram** cep**eras** cep**erat** cep**eramus** cep**eratis** cep**erant**	cep**ero** cep**eris** cep**erit** cep**erimus** cep**eritis** cep**erint**
4	audi**o** audi**s** audi**t** audi**mus** audi**tis** audi**unt**	audie**bam** audie**bas** audie**bat** audie**bamus** audie**batis** audie**bant**	audi**am** audi**es** audi**et** audi**emus** audi**etis** audi**ent**	audivi audiv**isti** audiv**it** audiv**imus** audiv**istis** audiv**erunt**	audiv**eram** audiv**eras** audiv**erat** audiv**eramus** audiv**eratis** audiv**erant**	audiv**ero** audiv**eris** audiv**erit** audiv**erimus** audiv**eritis** audiv**erint**

ACTIVE

Subjunctive

Group	Present	Imperfect	Perfect	Pluperfect
1	portem portes portet portemus portetis portent	portarem portares portaret portaremus portaretis portarent	portaverim portaveris portaverit portaverimus portaveritis portaverint	portavissem portavisses portavisset portavissemus portavissetis portavissent
2	habeam habeas habeat habeamus habeatis habeant	haberem haberes haberet haberemus haberetis haberent	habuerim habueris habuerit habuerimus habueritis habuerint	habuissem habuisses habuisset habuissemus habuissetis habuissent
3	mittam mittas mittat mittamus mittatis mittant	mitterem mitteres mitteret mitteremus mitteretis mitterent	miserim miseris miserit miserimus miseritis miserint	misissem misisses misisset misissemus misissetis misissent
	capiam capias capiat capiamus capiatis capiant	caperem caperes caperet caperemus caperetis caperent	ceperim ceperis ceperit ceperimus ceperitis ceperint	cepissem cepisses cepisset cepissemus cepissetis cepissent
4	audiam audias audiat audiamus audiatis audiant	audirem audires audiret audiremus audiretis audirent	audiverim audiveris audiverit audiverimus audiveritis audiverint	audivissem audivisses audivisset audivissemus audivissetis audivissent

PASSIVE

Indicative

Group	Present	Imperfect	Future	Perfect	Pluperfect	Future Perfect
1	port**or** portar**is** porta**tur** porta**mur** porta**mini** porta**ntur**	porta**bar** porta**baris** porta**batur** porta**bamur** porta**bamini** porta**bantur**	porta**bor** porta**beris** porta**bitur** porta**bimur** porta**bimini** porta**buntur**	portatus sum portatus es portatus est portati sumus portati estis portati sunt	portatus eram portatus eras portatus erat portati eramus portati eratis portati erant	portatus ero portatus eris portatus erit portati erimus portati eritis portati erunt
2	habe**or** habe**ris** habe**tur** habe**mur** habe**mini** habe**ntur**	habe**bar** habe**baris** habe**batur** habe**bamur** habe**bamini** habe**bantur**	habe**bor** habe**beris** habe**bitur** habe**bimur** habe**bimini** habe**buntur**	habitus sum habitus es habitus est habiti sumus habiti estis habiti sunt	habitus eram habitus eras habitus erat habiti eramus habiti eratis habiti erant	habitus ero habitus eris habitus erit habiti erimus habiti eritis habiti erunt
3	mitt**or** mitte**ris** mitti**tur** mitti**mur** mitti**mini** mitt**untur**	mitte**bar** mitte**baris** mitte**batur** mitte**bamur** mitte**bamini** mitte**bantur**	mitt**ar** mitte**ris** mitte**tur** mitte**mur** mitte**mini** mitte**ntur**	missus sum missus es missus est missi sumus missi estis missi sunt	missus eram missus eras missus erat missi eramus missi eratis missi erant	missus ero missus eris missus erit missi erimus missi eritis missi erunt
	capi**or** cape**ris** capi**tur** capi**mur** capi**mini** capi**untur**	capie**bar** capie**baris** capie**batur** capie**bamur** capie**bamini** capie**bantur**	capi**ar** capi**eris** capi**etur** capi**emur** capi**emini** capi**entur**	captus sum captus es captus est capti sumus capti estis capti sunt	captus eram captus eras captus erat capti eramus capti eratis capti erant	captus ero captus eris captus erit capti erimus capti eritis capti erunt
4	audi**or** audi**ris** audi**tur** audi**mur** audi**mini** audi**untur**	audie**bar** audie**baris** audie**batur** audie**bamur** audie**bamini** audie**bantur**	audi**ar** audi**eris** audi**etur** audi**emur** audi**emini** audi**entur**	auditus sum auditus es auditus est auditi sumus auditi estis auditi sunt	auditus eram auditus eras auditus erat auditi eramus auditi eratis auditi erant	auditus ero auditus eris auditus erit auditi erimus auditi eritis auditi erunt

Subjunctive

Group	Present	Imperfect	Perfect	Pluperfect
1	porter porteris portetur portemur portemini portentur	portarer portareris portaretur portaremur portaremini portarentur	portatus sim portatus sis portatus sit portati simus portati sitis portati sint	portatus essem portatus esses portatus esset portati essemus portati essetis portati essent
2	habear habearis habeatur habeamur habeamini habeantur	haberer habereris haberetur haberemur haberemini haberentur	habitus sim habitus sis habitus sit habiti simus habiti sitis habiti sint	habitus essem habitus esses habitus esset habiti essemus habiti essetis habiti essent
3	mittar mittaris mittatur mittamur mittamini mittantur	mitterer mittereris mitteretur mitteremur mitteremini mitterentur	missus sim missus sis missus sit missi simus missi sitis missi sint	missus essem missus esses missus esset missi essemus missi essetis missi essent
	capiar capiaris capiatur capiamur capiamini capiantur	caperer capereris caperetur caperemur caperemini caperentur	captus sim captus sis captus sit capti simus capti sitis capti sint	captus essem captus esses captus esset capti essemus capti essetis capti essent
4	audiar audiaris audiatur audiamur audiamini audiantur	audirer audireris audiretur audiremur audiremini audirentur	auditus sim auditus sis auditus sit auditi simus auditi sitis auditi sint	auditus essem auditus esses auditus esset auditi essemus auditi essetis auditi essent

ACTIVE

	Participle	Infinitive	Imperative
Present	port**ans**	port**are**	port**a** port**ate**
Future Perfect	portat**urus** —	portat**urus esse** porta**visse**	— —
Present	hab**ens**	hab**ere**	habe**e** hab**ete**
Future Perfect	habit**urus** —	habit**urus esse** habu**isse**	— —
Present	mitt**ens**	mitt**ere**	mitt**e** mitt**ite**
Future Perfect	miss**urus** —	miss**urus esse** mis**isse**	— —
Present	capi**ens**	cap**ere**	cap**e** cap**ite**
Future Perfect	capt**urus** —	capt**urus esse** cep**isse**	— —
Present	audi**ens**	aud**ire**	aud**i** aud**ite**
Future Perfect	audit**urus** —	audit**urus esse** audi**visse**	— —

PASSIVE

	Participle	Infinitive	Imperative
Present	—	portari	portare
			portamini
Future	—	portatum iri	—
Perfect	portatus	portatus esse	—
Present	—	haberi	habere
			habemini
Future	—	habitum iri	—
Perfect	habitus	habitus esse	—
Present	—	mitti	mittere
			mittimini
Future	—	missum iri	—
Perfect	missus	missus esse	—
Present	—	capi	capere
			capimini
Future	—	captum iri	—
Perfect	captus	captus esse	—
Present	—	audiri	audire
			audimini
Future	—	auditum iri	—
Perfect	auditus	auditus esse	—

IRREGULAR VERBS

Indicative

	Present	Imperfect	Future	Perfect	Pluperfect	Future Perfect
esse	sum	eram	ero	fui	fueram	fuero
	es	eras	eris	fuisti	fueras	fueris
	est	erat	erit	fuit	fuerat	fuerit
	sumus	eramus	erimus	fuimus	fueramus	fuerimus
	estis	eratis	eritis	fuistis	fueratis	fueritis
	sunt	erant	erunt	fuerunt	fuerant	fuerint
posse	possum	poteram	potero	potui	potueram	potuero
	potes	poteras	poteris	potuisti	potueras	potueris
	potest	poterat	poterit	potuit	potuerat	potuerit
	possumus	poteramus	poterimus	potuimus	potueramus	potuerimus
	potestis	poteratis	poteritis	potuistis	potueratis	potueritis
	possunt	poterant	poterunt	potuerunt	potuerant	potuerint
velle	volo	volebam	volam	volui	volueram	voluero
	vis	volebas	voles	voluisti	volueras	volueris
	vult	volebat	volet	voluit	voluerat	voluerit
	volumus	volebamus	volemus	voluimus	volueramus	voluerimus
	vultis	volebatis	voletis	voluistis	volueratis	volueritis
	volunt	volebant	volent	voluerunt	voluerant	voluerint
nolle	nolo	nolebam	nolam	nolui	nolueram	noluero
	nonvis	nolebas	noles	noluisti	nolueras	nolueris
	nonvult	nolebat	nolet	noluit	noluerat	noluerit
	nolumus	nolebamus	nolemus	noluimus	nolueramus	noluerimus
	nonvultis	nolebatis	noletis	noluistis	nolueratis	nolueritis
	nolunt	nolebant	nolent	noluerunt	noluerant	noluerint
malle	malo	malebam	malam	malui	malueram	maluero
	mavis	malebas	males	maluisti	malueras	malueris
	mavult	malebat	malet	maluit	maluerat	maluerit
	malumus	malebamus	malemus	maluimus	malueramus	maluerimus
	mavultis	malebatis	maletis	maluistis	malueratis	malueritis
	malunt	malebant	malent	maluerunt	maluerant	maluerint

Although these are called Irregular Verbs, they have many features
in common with regular verbs:
(a) the person endings;
(b) the Perfect, Pluperfect and Future Perfect are regular;
(c) the Imperfect Subjunctive is formed from the Present Infinitive
and the person endings;
(d) the Imperfect Indicative -bam, -bas, -bat, etc. is regular; (-ram,
-ras, -rat, etc. is not unlike this);
(e) -ro, -ris, -rit, etc. is not unlike -bo, -bis, -bit, etc.

Subjunctive

	Present	Imperfect		Perfect	Pluperfect
esse	sim	essem		fuerim	fuissem
	sis	esses		fueris	fuisses
	sit	esset		fuerit	fuisset
	simus	essemus		fuerimus	fuissemus
	sitis	essetis		fueritis	fuissetis
	sint	essent		fuerint	fuissent
posse	possim	possem		potuerim	potuissem
	possis	posses		potueris	potuisses
	possit	posset		potuerit	potuisset
	possimus	possemus		potuerimus	potuissemus
	possitis	possetis		potueritis	potuissetis
	possint	possent		potuerint	potuissent

	Participle	Infinitive	Imperative
Present	—	esse	es
			este
Future	futurus	futurus esse*	—
Perfect	—	fuisse	—
Present	—	posse	—
Future	—	—	—
Perfect	—	potuisse	—

*__fore__ is an alternative form of __futurus esse__ in all of its forms.

	Present	Imperfect		Perfect	Pluperfect
velle	velim	vellem		voluerim	voluissem
	velis	velles		volueris	voluisses
	velit	vellet		voluerit	voluisset
	velimus	vellemus		voluerimus	voluissemus
	velitis	velletis		volueritis	voluissetis
	velint	vellent		voluerint	voluissent
nolle	nolim	nollem		noluerim	noluissem
	nolis	nolles		nolueris	noluisses
	nolit	nollet		noluerit	noluisset
	nolimus	nollemus		noluerimus	noluissemus
	nolitis	nolletis		nolueritis	noluissetis
	nolint	nollent		noluerint	noluissent
malle	malim	mallem		maluerim	maluissem
	malis	malles		malueris	maluisses
	malit	mallet		maluerit	maluisset
	malimus	mallemus		maluerimus	maluissemus
	malitis	malletis		malueritis	maluissetis
	malint	mallent		maluerint	maluissent

	Participle	Infinitive	Imperative
Present	volens	velle	—
Future	—	—	—
Perfect	—	voluisse	—
Present	nolens	nolle	noli
			nolite
Future	—	—	—
Perfect	—	noluisse	—
Present	—	malle	—
Future	—	—	—
Perfect	—	maluisse	—

Indicative

	Present	Imperfect	Future	Perfect	Pluperfect	Future Perfect
ire	eo	ibam	ibo	ivi	iveram	ivero
	is	ibas	ibis	ivisti	iveras	iveris
	it	ibat	ibit	ivit	iverat	iverit
	imus	ibamus	ibimus	ivimus	iveramus	iverimus
	itis	ibatis	ibitis	ivistis	iveratis	iveritis
	eunt	ibant	ibunt	iverunt	iverant	iverint

	Present	Imperfect	Future	Perfect	Pluperfect	Future Perfect
fieri	fio	fiebam	fiam	factus sum	factus eram	factus ero
	fis	fiebas	fies	factus es	factus eras	factus eris
	fit	fiebat	fiet	factus est	factus erat	factus erit
	(fimus)	fiebamus	fiemus	facti sumus	facti eramus	facti erimus
	(fitis)	fiebatis	fietis	facti estis	facti eratis	facti eritis
	fiunt	fiebant	fient	facti sunt	facti erant	facti erunt

Subjunctive

	Present	Imperfect	Perfect	Pluperfect
ire	eam	irem	iverim	ivissem
	eas	ires	iveris	ivisses
	eat	iret	iverit	ivisset
	eamus	iremus	iverimus	ivissemus
	eatis	iretis	iveritis	ivissetis
	eant	irent	iverint	ivissent

	Participle	Infinitive	Imperative
Present	iens, euntis	ire	i
			ite
Future	iturus	iturus esse	—
Perfect	—	ivisse	—

	Present	Imperfect	Perfect	Pluperfect
fieri	fiam	fierem	factus sim	factus essem
	fias	fieres	factus sis	factus esses
	fiat	fieret	factus sit	factus esset
	fiamus	fieremus	facti simus	facti essemus
	fiatis	fieretis	facti sitis	facti essetis
	fiant	fierent	facti sint	facti essent

	Participle	Infinitive	Imperative
Present	—	fieri	—
Future	—	factum iri	—
Perfect	factus	factus esse	—

ACTIVE

Indicative

	Present	Imperfect	Future
ferre	fero fers fert ferimus fertis ferunt	ferebam ferebas ferebat ferebamus ferebatis ferebant	feram feres feret feremus feretis ferent

Perfect	Pluperfect	Future Perfect
tuli tulisti tulit tulimus tulistis tulerunt	tuleram tuleras tulerat tuleramus tuleratis tulerant	tulero tuleris tulerit tulerimus tuleritis tulerint

Subjunctive

Present	Imperfect	Perfect	Pluperfect
feram feras ferat feramus feratis ferant	ferrem ferres ferret ferremus ferretis ferrent	tulerim tuleris tulerit tulerimus tuleritis tulerint	tulissem tulisses tulisset tulissemus tulissetis tulissent

	Participle	Infinitive	Imperative
Present	ferens	ferre	fer ferte
Future	laturus	laturus esse	—
Perfect	—	tulisse	—

PASSIVE

Indicative

Present	Imperfect	Future
feror ferris fertur ferimur ferimini feruntur	ferebar ferebaris ferebatur ferebamur ferebamini ferebantur	ferar fereris feretur feremur feremini ferentur

Perfect	Pluperfect	Future Perfect
latus sum latus es latus est lati sumus lati estis lati sunt	latus eram latus eras latus erat lati eramus lati eratis lati erant	latus ero latus eris latus erit lati erimus lati eritis lati erunt

Subjunctive

Present	Imperfect
ferar feraris feratur feramur feramini ferantur	ferrer ferreris ferretur ferremur ferremini ferrentur

Perfect	Pluperfect
latus sim latus sis latus sit lati simus lati sitis lati sint	latus essem latus esses latus esset lati essemus lati essetis lati essent

	Participle	Infinitive	Imperative
Present	—	ferri	ferre ferimini
Future	—	latum iri	—
Perfect	latus	latus esse	—

DEPONENT VERBS

These verbs have mainly *passive* forms but *active* meanings.
There are only *three* principal parts, e.g.

Present	Infinitive	Perfect	Meaning
moro**r** sequo**r**	mor**ari** sequ**i**	mor**atus sum** sec**utus sum**	to delay to follow

Indicative:

Present	sequo**r**	I follow	Perfect	sec**utus sum**	I have followed
Imperfect	seque**bar**	I was following	Pluperfect	sec**utus eram**	I had followed
Future	sequ**ar**	I shall follow	Fut. Perf.	sec**utus ero**	I shall have followed

Subjunctive:

Present	sequ**ar**		Perfect	sec**utus sim**
Imperfect	seque**rer**		Pluperfect	sec**utus essem**

Participle:

Present	sequ**ens**	following
Future	sec**uturus**	about to follow
Perfect	sec**utus**	having followed

Infinitive:

Present	sequ**i**	to follow
Future	sec**uturus esse**	to be about to follow
Perfect	sec**utus esse**	to have followed

Imperative:

sequ**ere** sequ**imini**	} follow!

128

SEMI-DEPONENT VERBS

A few verbs are deponent only in the perfect, pluperfect and future perfect tenses. These are called semi-deponent verbs.

audeo	audere (2)	ausus sum	to dare
gaudeo	gaudere (2)	gavisus sum	to be glad
soleo	solere (2)	solitus sum	to be accustomed
fido	fidere (3)	fisus sum	to trust
confido	confidere (3)	confisus sum	to trust
diffido	diffidere (3)	diffisus sum	to distrust

DEFECTIVE VERBS

Defective verbs have no present, imperfect or future forms. These tenses are supplied by the perfect, pluperfect and future perfect.

Indicative:

memini	I remember	odi	I hate	novi	I know
memineram	I remembered	oderam	I hated	noveram	I knew
meminero	I shall remember	odero	I shall hate	novero	I shall know

Subjunctive:

meminerim	oderim	noverim
meminissem	odissem	novissem

Participle:

—	osurus about to hate	—

Infinitive:

meminisse to remember	odisse to hate	novisse to know

Imperative:

memento mementote } remember!

Vocabulary

A

a, ab (+ *abl.*), by, from, away from
abdo (3), **abdidi, abditum,** to hide
abeo, -ire, -ii, -itum, to go away, leave
abhinc (+ *acc.*), ago
abripio (3), **-ripui, -reptum,** to carry off, snatch
abstraho (3), **-traxi, -tractum,** to drag off
absum, abesse, afui, to be away, be distant
ac, and
accedo (3), **-cessi, -cessum,** to approach, come up to
accidit (3), **accidit,** it happens
accipio (3), **-cepi, -ceptum,** to receive, welcome
accipiter, -tris (*m*), hawk
accumbo (3), **-cubui, -cubitum,** to recline (at table)
accurro (3), **-curri, -cursum,** to run towards, run up to
accuso (1), to accuse
acies, -ei (*f*), line (of battle)
ad (+ *acc.*), to, towards, at, near
addo (3), **addidi, additum,** to add
adeo, to such a degree, so much, so
adeo, -ire, -ii, -itum, to go to, approach
adhaereo (2), **-haesi, -haesum,** to stick to
adhuc, still
adicio (3), **-ieci, -iectum,** to throw up, build near
adimo (3), **-emi, -emptum** (+ *dat.*), to take away (from)
adiuvo (1), **-iuvi, -iutum,** to help
admirationi esse, to be a source of wonder
admitto (3), **-misi, -missum,** to give an audience to, commit
adulescens, -entis (*m*), young man, youth
advenio (4), **-veni, -ventum,** to come to, reach, arrive (at)
adversarius, -i (*m*), opponent
adversus (+ *acc.*), against, in response to
advolo (1), to fly towards
aedificium, -i (*n*), building
aedilis, -is (*m*), aedile (a junior city magistrate)
Aeneis, -idis (*f*), the *Aeneid*
aequalis, -is, -e, equal, of the same age
aequus, -a, -um, equal, level
aes, aeris (*n*), bronze
aestas, -atis (*f*), summer
aestimo (1), to value
aeternus, -a, -um, eternal, everlasting
affectus, -a, -um, weakened, affected
affero, -ferre, attuli, allatum, to bring to, bring
ager, agri (*m*), field; (*pl.* territory)
agger, aggeris (*m*), rampart
aggredior (3), **-gressus sum,** to attack, approach
agmen, -inis (*n*), line of march, (army) column
agnus, -i (*m*), lamb
ago (3), **egi, actum,** to do, drive, discuss
   vitam agere, to spend one's life
ait, he/she says
ala, -ae (*f*), wing, squadron (of cavalry)
alacer, -cris, -cre, swift, keen
albus, -a, -um, white
alea, -ae (*f*), (gaming) die, dice
alias, at another time
alibi, elsewhere
alienus, -a, -um, belonging to another
aliquis, -quid, someone, something
alius, -a, -ud, another
   alii ... alii ..., some ... others ...
alloquor (3), **-locutus sum,** to speak to

almus, -a, -um, kindly
alo (3), **alui, altum,** to nourish
alter, -era, -erum, the other, the second, the one
altus, -a, -um, high, deep
amator, -oris (*m*), lover
ambiguus, -a, -um, doubtful
ambo, -ae, -o, both
ambulo (1), to walk
amica, -ae (*f*), friend
amice, in a friendly way
amicus, -i (*m*), friend
amitto (3), **-misi, -missum,** to lose
amo (1), to love
amor, -oris (*m*), love
amoveo (2), **amovi, amotum,** to move away
amphitheatrum, -i (*n*), amphitheatre
amplector (3), **amplexus sum,** to embrace
amplius, more
amplus, -a, -um, abundant
ancilla, -ae (*f*), maidservant, servant-girl
ancora, -ae (*f*), anchor
andron, -onis (*m*), passage
angelus, -i (*m*), messenger, angel
anima, -ae (*f*), breath, soul
animal, -alis (*n*), animal
animus, -i (*m*), mind, spirit, will
   animo deiectus, dispirited
   in animo habere, to intend
annuntio (1), to announce, proclaim
annus, -i (*m*), year
ante (+ *acc.*), before, in front of
antea, previously
antecedo (3), **-cessi, -cessum,** to go before, precede
anulus, -i (*m*), ring
aperio (4), **aperui, apertum,** to open
apertus, -a, -um, open
apodyterium, -i (*n*), changing room
appareo (2), to appear
apparitor, -oris (*m*), attendant
appello (1), to call, name
appropinquo (+ *dat.*, or **ad** + *acc.*), to approach, draw near
   (to)
aqua, -ae (*f*), water
aquarium, -i (*n*), watering place (for cattle)
aquarius, -i (*m*), water-carrier
aquila, -ae (*f*), eagle
aquilifer, -i (*m*), standard-bearer
arbiter, -tri (*m*), judge
arbitror (1), to think
arbor, -oris (*f*), tree
arceo (2), to obstruct, keep away
arcesso (3), **-ivi, -itum,** to send for, summon
ardeo (2), **arsi, arsum,** to burn
arduus, -a, -um, hard, difficult
area, -ae (*f*), courtyard
arena, -ae (*f*), arena, racecourse
argentarius, -i (*m*), silver-smith, money-changer
argentum, -i (*n*), silver
aries, -etis (*m*), battering-ram
arma, -orum (*n.pl*), arms, weapons
armatus, -a, -um, armed
ars, artis (*f*), art, skill
arx, arcis (*f*), citadel, fortress

asinus, -i (*m*), ass
at, but
atque, and
atrium, -i (*n*), atrium, main room
atrociter, fiercely
atrox, atrocis, frightful, harsh
attente, attentively
attentus, -a, -um, attentive
attonitus, -a, -um, astonished, thunderstruck
audax, -acis, bold
audeo (2), **ausus sum,** to dare
audio (4), to hear, listen to
aufero, -ferre, abstuli, ablatum, to take away, carry away
aufugio (3), **aufugi,** to run away, escape
aura, -ae (*f*), air, breeze
aureus, -a, -um, golden
auriga, -ae (*m*), charioteer
aurum, -i (*n*), gold
auspex, -icis (*m*), soothsayer
aut, or
   aut . . . aut . . ., either . . . or . . .
autem, however, but, moreover, now
auxilium, -i (*n*), help
  auxilio esse (+ *dat.*), to be of assistance (to), help
ave! avete! hail! greetings!
averto (3), **-verti, -versum,** to turn away
avis, avis (*f*), bird

B

baculum, -i (*n*), stick
Baiae, -arum (*f.pl*), Baiae
ballista, -ae (*f*), catapult
balneae, -arum (*f.pl*), baths
barbari, -orum (*m.pl*), the natives
beatus, -a, -um, happy
bellum, -i (*n*), war
bene, well
bestiarius, -i (*m*), a beast-fighter
bibo (3), **bibi,** to drink
biduanus, -a, -um, lasting two days
bis, twice
blandus, -a, -um, charming
bona, -orum (*n.pl*), goods, possessions
bonus, -a, -um, good
  bono esse (+ *dat.*), to be of advantage (to), benefit
bos, bovis (*m/f*), ox/cow
bracae, -arum (*f.pl*), breeches
brevis, -is, -e, short
  brevi tempore, in a short time
Britannia, -ae (*f*), Britain
Brundisium, -i (*n*), Brindisi

C

cadaver, -eris (*n*), corpse, body
cado (3), **cecidi, casum,** to fall
caelestis, -is, -e, heavenly, pertaining to the gods
caelum, -i (*n*), heaven, sky
caldarium, -i (*n*), hot-room
calidus, -a, -um, hot
caliga, -ae (*f*), boot
campus, -i (*m*), plain, level ground
canis, -is (*m/f*), dog
Cannae, -arum (*f.pl*), Cannae
capio (3), **cepi, captum,** to take, capture
  consilium capere, to form (adopt) a plan
Capitolium, -i (*n*), the Capitol
captivus, -i (*m*), prisoner
caput, capitis (*n*), head

carmen, -inis (*n*), song
caro, carnis (*f*), meat, flesh
carpo (3), **carpsi, carptum,** to gather, harvest, enjoy
Carthago, -inis (*f*), Carthage
carus, -a, -um, dear
castigo (1), to rebuke, reprimand
castra, -orum (*n.pl*), camp
catena, -ae (*f*), chain
caterva, -ae (*f*), crowd
caupo, -onis (*m*), innkeeper
caupona, -ae (*f*), inn
causa, -ae (*f*), reason, excuse, pretext
  genitive + **causa,** for the sake of
  causa indicta, without trial
caverna, -ae (*f*), hollow, crack, nook
cedo (3), **cessi, cessum,** to yield, give way
celer, -is, -e, swift, fast
celeritas, -atis (*f*), speed
  summa celeritate, as fast as possible
celeriter, quickly
  quam celerrime, as fast as possible
celo (1), to hide, conceal
cena, -ae (*f*), dinner
censor, -oris (*m*), censor, magistrate in charge of census
centum, hundred
centurio, -onis (*m*), centurion
certe, at least, certainly
certus, -a, -um, sure, certain
  pro certo habere, to be sure
cervix, -icis (*f*), neck
cervus, -i (*m*), stag
ceteri, -ae, -a, the rest, the others
  et cetera, and the rest
cibus, -i (*m*), food
circiter, about
circum (+ *acc.*), round, around
circumspicio (3), **-spexi, -spectum,** to look around
Circus, -i (*m*), the Circus Maximus
cista, -ae (*f*), chest, trunk
cithara, -ae (*f*), cithara, lute, guitar
cito, quickly
civis, -is (*m*), citizen
civitas, -atis (*f*), state, city
clam, secretly
clamo (1), to shout, cry, call
clamor, -oris (*m*), shout, shouting, noise
clarus, -a, -um, clear, famous, distinguished
classis, -is (*f*), fleet
claudo (3), **clausi, clausum,** to shut, enclose
clementer, quietly, gently
cliens, clientis (*m*), client, dependant
coepi, -isse, I began, have begun
cogito (1), to think, ponder over
cognomen, -inis (*n*), nickname
cognosco (3), **-novi, -nitum,** to learn, find out
cogo (3), **coegi, coactum,** to compel, gather, assemble
cohors, -ortis (*f*), cohort
collabor (3), **-lapsus sum,** to fall in ruins, fall in
collis, -is (*m*), hill
colloquor (3), **-locutus sum,** to converse with, talk
comes, -itis (*m*), companion
comiter, affably, amiably
comitia, -orum (*n.pl*), elections
commissum, -i (*n*), action, deed
commoror (1), to delay
commotus, -a, -um, moved
commoveo (2), **-movi, -motum,** to move
complector (3), **complexus sum,** to embrace

complures, -es, -a, several
compono (3), **-posui, -positum,** to put together, compose
concurro (3). **-curri, -cursum,** to run together, rush up
condicio, -onis (*f*), condition, stipulation
condo (3), **-didi, -ditum,** to found
conduco (3), **-duxi, -ductum,** to hire
confiteor (2), **-fessus sum,** to confess, admit
conflictus, -us (*m*), fight, contest
confugio (3), **-fugi,** to flee for refuge
conicio (3), **-ieci, -iectum,** to throw, hurl
coniunx, -iugis (*m/f*), husband/wife, spouse
conor (1), to try, attempt
conscientia, -ae (*f*), conscience
conscius, -a, -um, conscious, aware
consensus, -us (*m*), agreement
consentio (4), **-sensi, -sensum,** to agree
consequor (3), **-secutus sum,** to catch up, overtake
considero (1), to consider, reflect
consido (3), **-sedi, -sessum,** to sit down
consilium, -i (*n*), plan, advice
  consilium capere, to form (adopt) a plan
consisto (3), **-stiti,** to halt, stop, stand still
conspectus, -us (*m*), sight
conspicio (3), **-spexi, -spectum,** to catch sight of
conspicor (1), to see, notice
constat, it is agreed
constituo (3), **-ui, -utum,** to decide, draw up
  die constituta, on the appointed day
consul, -ulis (*m*), consul
consulo (3), **-sului, -sultum,** to consult
consultum, -i (*n*), decree
consumo (3), **-sumpsi, -sumptum,** to spend, use up
contendo (3), **-tendi, -tentum,** to strive, hasten, fight
contineo (2), **-tinui, -tentum,** to confine, hold (together)
contingit ut, it happens that
contio, -onis (*f*), meeting, assembly
contra (+ *acc.*), against, opposite; on the other hand, in reply
convalesco (3), **-valui,** to get well, grow stronger
convenio (4), **-veni, -ventum,** to come together, meet, assemble
converto (3), **-verti, -versum,** to turn, turn round
conviva, -ae (*m*), guest (at banquet)
coorior (4), **coortus sum,** to arise, rise, break out
copiae, -arum (*f.pl*), forces, supplies
coquo (3), **coxi, coctum,** to cook
coquus, -i (*m*), cook
cornu, -us (*n*), horn, wing (of an army)
corpus, -oris (*n*), body
corrigo (3), **-rexi, -rectum,** to correct, reform
corripio (3), **-ripui, -reptum,** to seize hold of
corvus, -i (*m*), crow, raven
cotidie, daily, every day
cras, tomorrow
creber, -bra, -brum, tightly-packed, numerous, many
credo (3), **credidi, -ditum** (+ *dat.*), to believe, trust
creo (1), to create, appoint
crinis, -is (*m*), hair
crocus, -i (*m*), crocus
cruciatus, -us (*m*), torture
crudelis, -is, -e, cruel
crudelitas, -atis (*f*), cruelty
cruentatus, -a, -um, covered in blood
crus, cruris (*n*), leg
cubiculum, -i (*n*), bedroom
culina, -ae (*f*), kitchen
culpa, -ae (*f*), blame, fault
culpo (1), to blame

cum (+ *abl.*), with
cum, when, since, although, whenever
cunabula, -orum, (*n.pl*), cradle
cunctus, -a, -um, all, whole
Cupido, -inis (*m*), Cupid (god of love)
cupidus, -a, -um, desirous (of), eager (to)
cupio (3), **cupivi, cupitum,** to wish, want, desire
cur, why
cura, -ae (*f*), anxiety
Curia, -ae (*f*), Senate-house
curo (1), to attend to, arrange
curriculum, -i (*n*), running, course
curro (3), **cucurri, cursum,** to run
cursus, -us (*m*), running, course, track
  cursus honorum, ladder of political advancement
custodio (4), to guard
custos, -odis (*m*), guard

D

de (+ *abl.*), from, down from, about, concerning
dea, -ae (*f*), goddess
debello (1), to defeat, conquer completely
decem, ten
decet, it is right
decimus, -a, -um, tenth
decipio (3), **-cepi, -ceptum,** to deceive
decorus, -a, -um, noble, fine, seemly
decurro (3), **-(cu)curri, -cursum,** to run down
dedecori esse (+ *dat.*), to be a cause of shame (to), bring disgrace (upon)
deduco (3), **-duxi, -ductum,** to bring, escort
deductio, -onis (*f*), procession
defendo (3), **-fendi, -fensum,** to defend
defero, -ferre, -tuli, -latum, to bring back, report
defessus, -a, -um, weary
deiectus animo, demoralised, dispirited
deinde, then
delecto (1), to delight
deleo (2), **-evi, -etum,** to destroy
deligo (1), to bind, anchor
deligo (3), **-legi, -lectum,** to choose, select
delphinus, -i (*m*), dolphin
demonstro (1), to show
demum, at last
dens, dentis (*m*), tooth
depono (3), **-posui, -positum,** to lay down, put aside
derideo (2), **-risi, -risum,** to laugh at, mock, scorn
descendo (3), **-scendi, -scensum,** to climb down
descensus, -us (*m*), descent
desero (3), **-serui, -sertum,** to desert, abandon
desertum, -i (*n*), wilderness, desert
desidero (1), to long for, miss, feel the lack of
desilio (4), **-silui, -sultum,** to leap down
desino (3), **-sii, -situm,** to cease, stop
desisto (3), **-stiti,** to cease, give up
despero (1), to despair, give up hope
despicio (3), **-spexi, -spectum,** to despise
deterritus, -a, -um, deterred, put off
detestatus, -a, -um, hated, detested
deus, -i (*m*), god
  di immortales, the immortal gods
devoro (1), to devour
dextra, -ae (*f*), right hand
dico (3), **dixi, dictum,** to say, tell
dies, -ei (*m*), day
  die constituta, on the appointed day
difficilis, -is, -e, difficult
diffido (3), **-fisus sum** (+ *dat.*), to distrust

dignitas, -atis (*f*), dignity, rank, status
digredior (3), **-gressus sum,** to depart
diligenter, carefully, diligently
diligo (3), **-lexi, -lectum,** to love
dimitto (3), **-misi, -missum,** to send away
discedo (3), **-cessi, -cessum,** to go away, depart
discipulus, -i (*m*), pupil
disco (3), **didici,** to learn
discrimen, -inis (*n*), danger, risk
discutio (3), **-cussi, -cussum,** to examine
disputatio, -onis (*f*), argument
disputo (1), to argue
diu, for a long time
diversicolor, -oris, of various colours
dives, divitis, rich
divido (3), **divisi, divisum,** to divide
divinus, -a, -um, divine
divitiae, -arum (*f.pl*), riches, wealth
divus, -a, -um, divine, deified
do (1), **dedi, datum,** to give, offer
doceo (2), **docui, doctum,** to teach
dolor, -oris (*m*), grief
domesticus, -a, -um, internal
domina, -ae (*f*), mistress
dominus, -i (*m*), master, Lord
domus, -us (*f*), house, home
   domi, at home
   domo, from home
   domum, home, homewards
donec, until
dono (1), to give as a present
donum, -i (*n*), gift
   dono dare, to give as a gift
dormio (4), to sleep
dos, dotis (*f*), dowry
dubito (1), to hesitate, have doubts
duco (3), **duxi, ductum,** to lead, take, bring, think, marry
dulcis, -is, -e, sweet
dum, while, as long as, provided that, until
duo, duae, duo, two
durus, -a, -um, hard, harsh
dux, ducis (*m*), leader, general

E

e, ex (+ *abl.*), out of, from
ecce! look! see!
edo (3), **edidi, editum,** to give out
edo, esse, edi, esum, to eat
effigies, -ei (*f*), likeness, image
effugio (3), **-fugi,** to escape
ego, I
egredior (3), **-gressus sum,** to go out, leave, disembark
egregie, excellently, very well
eheu! alas!
eicio (3), **eieci, eiectum,** to throw out
elephantus, -i (*m*), elephant
eludo, (3), **elusi, elusum,** to elude, mock, baffle, make sport of
emo (3), **emi, emptum,** to buy
enim, for
eo, ire, ivi (ii), itum, to go
eo, to that place, there
epigramma, -atis (*n*), inscription, epigram
epistola, -ae (*f*), letter
epistula, -ae (*f*), letter
equitatus, -us (*m*), cavalry
equites, -um (*m.pl*), cavalry, the *equites* (knights)
equus, -i (*m*), horse

ergo, therefore
erro (1), to wander, err, make a mistake
eruditus, -a, -um, learned, scholarly
essedarius, -i (*m*), chariot-warrior
essedum, -i (*n*), war-chariot
et, and, also, even
   et . . . et . . ., (both) . . . and . . .
etiam, also, even
everto (3), **everti, eversum,** to overturn, overthrow
excipio (3), **-cepi, -ceptum,** to receive, welcome
excito (1), to arouse
exclamo (1), to shout out, exclaim
excrucio (1), to torture
exemplum, -i (*n*), example
exeo, -ire, -ii, -itum, to go out, leave
exerceo (2), to exercise, train
exercitus, -us (*m*), army
exigo (3), **exegi, exactum,** to complete, finish, perfect
exitio esse (+ *dat.*), to bring about the destruction (of), to destroy
expello (3), **-puli, -pulsum,** to drive out, expel
expono (3), **-posui, -positum,** to lay out, land (troops), disembark
exprimo (3), **-pressi, -pressum,** to express
exspecto (1), to wait for, expect
exstinguo (3), **-stinxi, -stinctum,** to put out, eliminate, destroy
extraho (3), **-traxi, -tractum,** to drag out, pull out
exul, exulis (*m*), an exile
exuo (3), **exui, exutum,** to take off

F

fabula, -ae (*f*), story
facile, easily
facilis, -is, -e, easy
facio (3), **feci, factum,** to make, do
   iter facere, to journey
facultas, -atis (*f*), capability, opportunity
falcarius, -i (*m*), sickle-maker
falsus, -a, -um, false, made-up
falx, falcis (*f*), sickle
fama, -ae (*f*), gossip, rumour
fames, -is (*f*), hunger
familia, -ae (*f*), family, household
faveo (2), **favi, fautum** (+ *dat.*), to favour
feles, -is (*f*), cat
feliciter! good luck!
felix, -icis, happy, lucky, fortunate
femina, -ae (*f*), woman
fenestra, -ae (*f*), window
ferculum, -i (*n*), dish, tray, course (at dinner)
fere, almost, roughly
fero, ferre, tuli, latum, to carry, bear, bring
ferociter, fiercely
ferox, -ocis, fierce
ferus, -a, -um, wild
festino (1), to hurry, hasten
fidelis, -is, -e, faithful
fides, -ei (*f*), faith, loyalty, trust
filia, -ae (*f*), daughter
filius, -i (*m*), son
finio (4), to finish
finis, -is (*m*), end
   fines, -ium (*m.pl*), territory
fio, fieri, factus sum, to be made, become
flamma, -ae (*f*), flame
flammeum, -i (*n*), (flame-coloured) bridal veil
flecto (3), **flexi, flexum,** to turn

133

fleo (2), **flevi, fletum,** to weep
fletus, -us (*m*), weeping
floreo (2), to flower, bloom, flourish
flos, floris (*m*), flower
fluctus, -us (*m*), wave
flumen, -inis (*n*), river
fons, fontis (*m*), fountain, spring, pond
foras ire, to go out of doors
forsan, perhaps
fortasse, perhaps
forte, by chance, perchance, perhaps, as it happened
fortis, -is, -e, brave, strong
fortiter, bravely
fortuna, -ae (*f*), fortune, good luck
Forum, -i (*n*), Forum, market-place
fossa, -ae (*f*), ditch
fragor, -oris (*m*), crash
frango (3), **fregi, fractum,** to break
frater, fratris (*m*), brother
frequens, -entis, frequent, crowded, numerous, "en masse"
frico (1), **-ui, -ctum,** to rub
frigidarium, -i (*n*), cooling-room
frigidus, -a, -um, cold
frumentum, -i (*n*), corn
frustra, in vain
frustum, -i (*n*), piece, bit, scrap
fugio (3), **fugi,** to flee, run away, escape
fulgeo (2), **fulsi, fulsum,** to shine, flash, gleam
fumus, -i (*m*), smoke
funditor, -oris (*m*), slinger
fundus, -i (*m*), farm, farm-house
fur, furis (*m*), thief
furtim, stealthily
furtum, -i (*n*), theft

G

galea, -ae (*f*), helmet
gaudeo (2), **gavisus sum,** to rejoice
gaudium, -i (*n*), joy, happiness
gens, gentis (*f*), race, tribe, family, clan
genus, generis (*n*), kind, race, family
gero (3), **gessi, gestum,** to wear, carry on, wage
   rem bene gerere, to be successful
gigno (3), **genui, genitum,** to give birth to
gladiator, -oris (*m*), gladiator
gladius, -i (*m*), sword
gloria, -ae (*f*), glory, fame
gracilis, -is, -e, slender, unadorned
Graecus, -i (*m*), Greek
grammaticus, -i (*m*), teacher
gratia, -ae (*f*), favour, courtesy, thanks
   genitive + **gratia,** for the sake of
   gratias agere (+ *dat.*), to thank
   gratis (contracted from **gratiis**), free, for nothing
gratus, -a, -um, pleasing, welcome
gravis, -is, -e, heavy, serious
graviter, heavily, seriously
grus, gruis (*f*), crane
gustatio, -onis (*f*), first tasting of food, hors d'oeuvre

H

habeo (2), to have, hold
   in animo habere, to intend
   pro certo habere, to be sure
habito (1), to dwell, live
haereo (2), **haesi, haesum,** to stick, cling
haesito (1), to doubt, hesitate
haud, no, by no means

haurio (4), **hausi, haustum,** to drain, swallow up
herbarium, -i (*n*), collection of dried plants
hercle! by Hercules!
heres, -edis (*m*), heir
heri, yesterday
hiberna, -orum (*n.pl*), winter-quarters
hic, here
hic, haec, hoc, this
hiems, hiemis (*f*), winter
hilaris, -is, -e, cheerful, merry
hilaritas, -atis (*f*), good humour, merriment
hodie, today
homo, hominis (*m*), man, fellow, person
   homines, -um (*m.pl*), people
honestus, -a, -um, honourable, respected
honoro (1), to honour
honos, -oris (*m*), honour, political office
   honoris causa, as an honour
hora, -ae (*f*), hour
horrendus, -a, -um, terrifying, frightening
hortor (1), to encourage, urge
hospes, -itis (*m*), friend, guest
hospicium, -i (*n*), home
hostilis, -is, -e, hostile, enemy
hostis, -is (*m*), enemy
huc, hither, to this place
   huc illuc, here and there, hither and thither
humanus, -a, -um, human, connected with man
humus, -i (*f*), earth
hyacinthus, -i (*m*), hyacinth

I

iaceo (2), to lie
iacio (3), **ieci, iactum,** to throw
iacto (1), to throw, cast
iam, already, now
   iam diu, for a long time now
   iam pridem, long ago
ianua, -ae (*f*), door
ibi, there
idem, eadem, idem, the same
identidem, repeatedly, time and time again
idoneus, -a, -um, suitable
Idus, -uum (*f.pl*), Ides
ieiunus, -a, -um, without eating, hungry
igitur, therefore
ignavus, -a, -um, lazy, cowardly
ignis, -is (*m*), fire
ignoro (1), to be ignorant of, not to know
ille, illa, illud, that; he, she, it
imago, -inis (*f*), image, likeness, reflection
immanis, -is, -e, huge, monstrous, savage
immensus, a, -um, huge
immobilis, -is, -e, not able to move
immortalis, -is, -e, immortal
   di immortales, the immortal gods
impedimenta, -orum, (*n.pl*), baggage
impedio (4), to hinder
imperator, -oris (*m*), general, emperor
imperium, -i (*n*), power
impero (1) (+ *dat.*), to order, demand, levy
impetro (1), to have a request granted
impetus, -us (*m*), attack, fit (of anger)
impluvium, -i (*n*), impluvium (decorative basin)
improvisus, -a, -um, unforeseen, unexpected(ly)
in (+ *abl.*), in, on
in (+ *acc.*), into, to, against
incedo (3), **-cessi, -cessum,** to march, advance, strut about

incendium, -i (*n*), fire
incendo (3), **-cendi, -censum,** to burn, set on fire
incido (3), **-cidi, -casum,** to fall in
incipio (3), **-cepi, -ceptum,** to begin
incito (1), to spur on, rouse
incola, -ae (*m*), inhabitant, tenant
incolumis, -is, -e, safe
inde, from there
indicta causa, without a trial
induco (3), **-duxi, -ductum,** to lead in
induo (3), **-ui, -utum,** to put on
infelix, -icis, unlucky
infirmus, -a, -um, weak, shaky
infra (+ *acc.*), below
ingenium, -i (*n*), intelligence, ingenuity
ingens, -entis, huge, great, vast
ingredior (3), **-gressus sum,** to go on (in), enter
inicio (3), **-ieci, -iectum,** to throw into (upon), thrust
inimicus, -i (*m*), enemy
iniquus, -a, -um, unequal, unfair, unjust
innocens, -entis, innocent
inopia, -ae (*f*), scarcity, lack
inquit, he/she says (said)
insanus, -a, -um, mad, crazy
inscius, -a, -um, not knowing
insisto (3), **-stiti** (+ *dat.*), to stand upon
inspicio (3), **-spexi, -spectum,** to examine
instruo (3), **-struxi, -structum,** to draw up, set in order
insula, -ae (*f*), island, tenement
integer, -gra, -grum, whole, blameless, without blemishes
intellego (3), **-lexi, -lectum,** to realise, understand
inter (+ *acc.*), between, among
interea, meanwhile
interdiu, by day, during the day
interdum, sometimes
interficio (3), **-feci, -fectum,** to kill
interim, meanwhile
interimo (3), **-emi, -emptum,** to kill, destroy
interloquor (3), **-locutus sum,** to interrupt in speaking
interpello (1), to interrupt
interrogo (1), to ask, question
interrumpo (3), **-rupi, -ruptum,** to break through (down)
intra (+ *acc.*), inside, within
intrepidus, -a, -um, fearless
intro (1), to go into, enter
introeo, -ire, -ii, -itum, to enter
introitus, -us (*m*), entrance
intueor (2), **-tuitus sum,** to look at, see
invenio (4), **-veni, -ventum,** to come upon, find
invideo (2), **-vidi, -visum** (+ *dat.*), to envy
invito (1), to invite
invitus, -a, -um, unwilling(ly)
iocor (1), to jest, joke
iocus, -i (*m*), jest, funny story
ipse, ipsa, ipsum, -self
ira, -ae (*f*), anger
irascor (3), **iratus sum** (+ *dat.*), to be angry (with)
iratus, -a, -um, angry
is, ea, id, this, that; he, she, it
iste, that man, the accused
ita, in this way, in such a way, so, thus
itaque, and so, therefore
iter, itineris (*n*), journey, march
iter facere, to journey, travel, march
iterum, again
iubeo (2), **iussi, iussum,** to order
Iudaeus, -i (*m*), Jew
iudex, iudicis (*m*), judge

iudices, -um (*m.pl*), members of the jury
Iuppiter, Iovis (*m*), Jupiter
iuro (1), to take an oath, swear
ius, iuris (*n*), law, a right
iuvenis, -is (*m*), young man
iuventus, -utis (*f*), youth
iuvo (1), **iuvi, iutum,** to help, give pleasure

K
Kalendae, -arum (*f.pl*), Kalends

L
labor, -oris (*m*), work, task
laboro (1), to work, toil, be in difficulties
lacrima, -ae (*f*), tear
lacrimo (1), to weep
lacto (1), to feed with milk, suckle
laedo (3), **laesi, laesum,** to harm
laetitia, -ae (*f*), happiness, joy
laetus, -a, -um, happy, joyful
lanio (1), to tear at
lapideus, -a, -um, made of stone
lapis, lapidis (*m*), stone
lassus, -a, -um, weary, languid, exhausted
lateo (2), to be hidden, lie in hiding
latro (1), to bark
latus, -a, -um, wide, broad
latus, -eris (*n*), side
laudi esse (+ *dat.*), to be a credit to
laudo (1), to praise
lectica, -ae (*f*), litter
lecticarius, -i (*m*), litter-bearer
lectus, -i (*m*), bed, couch
legatus, -i (*m*), ambassador, staff-officer, general
legio, -onis (*f*), legion
legionarius, -i (*m*), legionary-soldier
lego (3), **legi, lectum,** to gather, collect, read
leo, leonis (*m*), lion
lepus, leporis (*m*), hare
levis, -is, -e, light, effortless
lex, legis (*f*), law
libenter, gladly, willingly
liber, -era, -erum, free
liber, libri (*m*), book
libri annales, archives, records
liberi, -orum (*m.pl*), children
libero (1), to set free
licet (+ *dat.*), it is allowed
mihi licet, I am allowed
lictor, -oris (*m*), lictor, attendant of magistrate
ligo (1), to bind, tie up
lilium, -i (*n*), lily
limen, -inis (*n*), threshold, doorway
liquor, -oris (*m*), liquid
litterae, -arum (*f.pl*), letter, dispatches
litus, -oris (*n*), shore, beach
locus, -i (*m*), place
longe, far
longus, -a, -um, long
loquor (3), **locutus sum,** to speak
Lotophagus, -i (*m*), Lotus-eater
luctus, -us, (*m*), grief, distress
ludo (3), **lusi, lusum,** to play
ludus, -i (*m*), game, school
luna, -ae (*f*), moon
lupus, -i (*m*), wolf
lux, lucis (*f*), light
prima luce, at dawn

M

magis, more
  eo magis, all the more
magister, -tri (*m*), teacher, (school)master
magnopere, greatly
magnus, -a, -um, large, great, loud
  magni (*gen. sing.*), highly
maiestas, -atis (*f*), majesty, dignity
male, badly
maledico (3), **-dixi, -dictum** (+ *dat.*), to abuse, curse
malo, malle, malui, to prefer
malum, -i (*n*), apple
malum, -i (*n*), evil, hardship
malus, -a, -um, wicked, bad
mandatum, -i (*n*), order, instruction
maneo (2), **mansi, mansum,** to remain
manes, -ium (*m.pl*), spirits of the dead, the departed spirit of a person
manifestus, -a, -um, obvious, evident
manus, -us (*f*), hand, band
  manum conserere, to engage in close combat, hand-to-hand fighting
mappa, -ae (*f*), napkin
mare, maris (*n*), sea
margarita, -ae (*f*), pearl
margaritarius, -i (*m*), pearl-fisher, dealer in pearls
maritimus, -a, -um, sea, naval
mater, matris (*f*), mother
matrimonium, -i (*n*), marriage
  in matrimonium ducere, to marry
matrona, -ae (*f*), married woman
maxime, very, very much, mostly
maximus, -a, -um, largest, very big
medius, -a, -um, mid-, middle of
memento! remember!
memoria, -ae (*f*), memory, recollection, tradition
memoro (1), to declare, relate, record
mens, mentis (*f*), mind, plan, intention
mensa, -ae (*f*), table
mensis, -is (*m*), month
meridianus, -a, -um, mid-day
meridies, -ei (*m*), mid-day
meta, -ae (*f*), mark, goal, turning post (in race)
metuo (3), **-ui,** to fear
metus, -us (*m*), fear
meus, -a, -um, my, mine
migro (1), to move one's home
miles, -itis (*m*), soldier
mille (*pl.* **milia**), thousand
mimarius, -i (*m*), a mimic actor, one who performs in mimes
minime, least, by no means, no
minor (1), to threaten
minus, less
mirabilis, -is, -e, wonderful
miraculum, -i (*n*), marvel, wonder
mirmillo, -onis (*m*), gladiator with fish emblem
miror (1), to wonder at, be surprised
mirus, -a, -um, wonderful
miser, -a, -um, unhappy, wretched
mitto (3), **misi, missum,** to send
mobilis, -is, -e, easy to move, movable
moderatio, -onis (*f*), moderation
modo, only
moenia, -ium (*n.pl*), (city) walls
mollis, -is, -e, soft, gentle
moneo (2), to warn, advise
mons, montis (*m*), mountain
monumentum, -i (*n*), monument

mora, -ae (*f*), delay
moratorius, -a, -um, delaying
morior (3), **mortuus sum,** to die
moror (1), to delay, remain
mors, mortis (*f*), death
morsus, -us (*m*), bite
mortuus, -a, -um, dead
mos, moris (*m*), custom, way, manner
moveo (2), **movi, motum,** to move
mox, soon
muliebris, -is, -e, of a woman, womanly, female
mulier, -eris (*f*), woman
multitudo, -inis (*f*), large number, crowd
multo (with *comparative*), much
multus, -a, -um, much
  multi, -ae, -a, many
mundus, -i (*m*), world, universe
munio (4), to fortify
munitio, -onis (*f*), fortification, defence
murus, -i (*m*), wall
mus, muris (*m*), mouse
mutabilis, -is, -e, changeable
muto (1), to change

N

nam, for
nanciscor (3), **nactus sum,** to obtain
narro (1), to tell, narrate
nascor (3), **natus sum,** to be born
nato (1), to swim
natura, -ae (*f*), nature
naumachia, -ae (*f*), mock sea-battle
nausea, -ae (*f*), sickness
nauta, -ae (*m*), sailor
navigo (1), to sail
navis, -is (*f*), ship
  navem solvere, to set sail
  navis longa, warship
-ne? (indicates a question)
ne (+ *subjunctive*), in case, lest, to avoid, that, that . . . not; do not!
ne . . . quidem, not even
Neapolis, -is (*f*), Naples
nec, and . . . not, nor
  nec . . . nec . . ., neither . . . nor . . .
necesse est, it is necessary
neco (1), to kill
neglegenter, carelessly
neglego (3), **-lexi, -lectum,** to neglect
nego (1), to say that . . . not, deny
negotiosus, -a, -um, busy
nemo, no one
neque, and . . . not, nor
  neque . . . neque . . ., neither . . . nor . . .
nescio (4), to be ignorant, not to know
niger, -gra, -grum, black
nihil, nothing
nil, nothing
nimius, -a, -um, excessive, too much
nisi, unless, if . . . not
nixus, -a, -um (+ *abl.*), relying (upon)
nobilis, -is, -e, noble
nocens, -entis, guilty
noceo (2) (+ *dat.*), to harm, injure
nolo, nolle, nolui, to be unwilling, refuse
nomen, -inis (*n*), name
non, not
Nonae, -arum (*f.pl*), Nones

nondum, not yet

nonne? surely?

nonnulli, -ae, -a, some, several

nonus, -a, -um, ninth

nos, we, us

noster, -tra, -trum, our
   nostri, -orum (*m.pl*), our men

noto (1), to mark, note, point out

notus, -a, -um, known, well-known

novem, nine

novus, -a, -um, new

nox, noctis (*f*), night

nubo (3), **nupsi, nuptum** (+ *dat.*), to marry

nudus, -a, -um, naked

nullus, -a, -um, no, none

num, surely . . . not? whether, if

numquam, never

nunc, now

nuntio (1), to announce, report

nuntius, -i (*m*), messenger

nuper, recently

nuptiae, -arum (*f.pl*), wedding

nusquam, nowhere

nux, nucis (*f*), nut

nympha, -ae (*f*), nymph, demi-goddess

O

ob (+ *acc.*), because of, on account of

obsecro (1), to beg, beseech

obsideo (2), **-sedi, -sessum,** to besiege, blockade

obstinatus, -a, -um, determined, stubborn, inflexible

obtineo (2), to obtain, have one's way

obturbo (1), to confuse, distract

obviam (+ *dat.*), in the way (of)
   obviam ire (+ *dat.*), to go to meet

occido (3), **-cidi, -cisum,** to kill

occupatus, -a, -um, busy

occupo (1), to seize, take possession of

occurro (3), **-curri, -cursum** (+ *dat.*), to run to meet, attack

octingenti, -ae, -a, 800

oculus, -i (*m*), eye

odi, -isse, to hate

odiosus, -a, -um, hateful, offensive

odium, -i (*n*), hatred
   odio esse, to be an object of hatred

offero, -ferre, obtuli, oblatum, to offer

olim, once upon a time, one day

omnis, -is, -e, all, every

onager, -i (*m*), military machine, siege engine

opera, -ae (*f*), work, efforts

operor (1), to work, labour, toil

oportet te (+ *infin.*), you must

oppidum, -i (*n*), town

opprimo (3), **-pressi, -pressum,** to crush, overwhelm

oppugno (1), to attack

optime, very well, excellently

optimus, -a, -um, excellent, very good, best

opus, operis (*n*), work, defence works

oraculum, -i (*n*), oracle

orator, -oris (*m*), orator, speaker

Orcus, -i (*m*), the Underworld, Hell

ordo, -inis (*m*), rank

orior (4), **ortus sum,** to rise, begin

orno (1), to decorate, equip

oro (1), to beg, pray

os, oris (*n*), face

os, ossis (*n*), bone

osculum, -i (*n*), kiss

ostendo (3), **-tendi, -tentum,** to show, point out

otium, -i (*n*), leisure

ovum, -i (*n*), egg

P

paene, almost

paenitentia, -ae (*f*), repentance, regret

paenitet me, I repent, regret

palaestra, -ae (*f*), exercise-area (mainly for wrestling)

pallidus, -a, -um, pale, pallid

panis, -is (*m*), bread
   panem et circenses, bread and circus shows (i.e. dole and entertainment)

paratus, -a, -um, prepared, ready

parco (3), **peperci, parsum** (+ *dat.*), to spare

parens, -entis (*m*), parent

pareo (2) (+ *dat.*), to obey

pario (3), **peperi, partum,** to bear (a child)

paro (1), to prepare

pars, partis (*f*), part

parvulus, -a, -um, tiny, very small

pasco (3), **pavi, pastum,** to pasture, graze

patefacio (3), **-feci, -factum,** to lay open, expose

pater, -tris (*m*), father
   patres, -um (*m.pl*), senators

patior (3), **passus sum,** to suffer, endure

patria, -ae (*f*), native land

pauci, -ae, -a, few, a few

paulatim, gradually, little by little

paulisper, for a short time

paulo (with *comparative*), a little

pauper, -eris, poor

pavimentum, -i (*n*), tiled floor

pax, pacis (*f*), peace

pecto (3), **pexi, pexum,** to comb

pecunia, -ae (*f*), money

pedites, -um (*m.pl*), infantry, foot-soldiers

peior, peius, worse

pello (3), **pepuli, pulsum,** to drive, push back, beat

penates, -ium (*m.pl*), household gods

penetro (1), to enter, penetrate

per (+ *acc.*), through, along, over

percutio (3), **-cussi, -cussum,** to strike

perdo (3), **-didi, -ditum,** to lose, destroy

perennis, -is, -e, everlasting

pereo, -ire, -ii, -itum, to perish

perfero, -ferre, -tuli, -latum, to convey, report, endure

perforo (1), to bore through

periculosus, -a, -um, dangerous

periculum, -i (*n*), danger

peristylium, -i (*n*), peristyle, garden

permitto (3), **-misi, -missum,** to allow, permit

permutatio, -onis (*f*), exchange

pernicies, -ei (*f*), destruction, losses

perpetuus, -a, -um, perpetual, continual, continuous

persevero (1), to persist, persevere

persona, -ae (*f*), character (in a play), person

persuadeo (2), **-suasi, -suasum** (+ *dat.*), to persuade

perterritus, -a, -um, terrified, very frightened

pertinax, -acis, determined, stubborn

perturbo (1), to disturb, throw into confusion

pervenio (4), **-veni, -ventum** (**ad** + *acc.*), to arrive (at), reach

pes, pedis (*m*), foot

pessime, worst, very badly

pessimus, -a, -um, worst, very bad

peto (3), **-ivi, -itum,** to seek, aim at, make for, attack

pilum, -i (*n*), javelin

pinguis, -is, -e, fat

piscina, -ae (*f*), pool
pius, -a, -um, devout, dutiful, good
placeo (2) (+ *dat.*), to please
placet (+ *dat.*), it is decided (by)
placide, quietly, tamely, calmly
plaustrum, -i (*n*), wagon
plebs, plebis (*f*), common-people
plenus, -a, -um, full
plus, more
Pluto, -onis (*m*), Pluto (god of the underworld)
Poeni, -orum (*m.pl*), Carthaginians
poeta, -ae (*m*), poet
pono (3), **posui, positum,** to place, put
pons, pontis (*m*), bridge
pontifex, -icis (*m*), priest
popina, -ae (*f*), café
populor (1), to plunder, ravage
populus, -i (*m*), people
porcus, -i (*m*), pig
porro, far off, furthermore
porticus, -us (*f*), colonnade, gallery
porto (1), to carry
portus, -us (*m*), harbour
posco (3), **poposci,** to ask for, demand
possum, posse, potui, to be able
post, afterwards, later
post (+ *acc.*), after, behind
postea, after that, afterwards
posterus, -a, -um, next, following
   posteri, -orum (*m.pl*), descendants
posticum, -i (*n*), back-door
postquam, after
postridie, on the following day
prae (+ *abl.*), on account of, because of
praecedo (3), **-cessi, -cessum,** to precede, go in front of, excel
praeceps, -cipitis, headlong, head-first
praecipio (3), **-cepi, -ceptum** (+ *dat.*), to instruct, order
praeclarus, -a, -um, famous, distinguished
praecludo (3), **-clusi, -clusum,** to block
praeda, -ae (*f*), booty, loot
praedo, -onis (*m*), robber, pirate
praefero, -ferre, -tuli, -latum (+ *dat.*), to prefer, value more highly (than)
praeficio (3), **-feci, -fectum** (+ *dat.*), to put in command (of)
praemium, -i (*n*), reward
praeparo (1), to get ready beforehand
praescribo (3), **-scripsi, -scriptum,** to direct, prescribe
praesens, -entis, present
praesidium, -i (*n*), garrison
   praesidio esse (+ *dat.*), to be a means of protection (to), to protect
praeter (+ *acc.*), except, past, beyond
praetercurro (3), to run past
praeterea, besides
praetereo, -ire, -ii, -itum, to go past, beyond
preces, -um (*f.pl*), prayers, pleas
prehendo (3), **-hendi, -hensum,** to seize
pretiosus, -a, -um, precious, expensive
pretium, -i (*n*), price
pridie, on the previous day, the day before
primo, at first
primum, first
primus, -a, -um, first
   prima luce, at dawn
princeps, -ipis (*m*), leading citizen, leader, emperor
prior, -oris, first (of two)
prius, previously

pro (+ *abl.*), in front of, on behalf of, for
probo (1), to approve
probus, -a, -um, honest, upright, honourable
procax, -acis, insolent, shameless
procedo (3), **-cessi, -cessum,** to advance
proceritas, -atis (*f*), height
procul, far, far off
prodeo, -ire, -ii, -itum, to come (go) forth
proelium, -i (*n*), battle
proficiscor (3), **profectus sum,** to set out
progredior (3), **-gressus sum,** to go forward, advance
prohibeo (2) (+ *infin.*), to prevent (from)
promitto (3), **-misi, -missum,** to promise
pronuba, -ae (*f*), bride's attendant
prope, near by, almost
prope (+ *acc.*), near
propono (3), **-posui, -positum,** to display, set before
propraetor, -oris (*n*), propraetor, governor
propter (+ *acc.*), on account of
propugnatio, -onis (*f*), defence, protection
propugno (1), to rush out to defend (fight)
prosequor (3), **-secutus sum,** to pursue
prospectus, -us (*m*), view
provincia, -ae (*f*), province
provoco (1), to call forth, challenge
proximus, -a, -um, next, nearest
prudens, -entis, wise, sensible
prudentia, -ae (*f*), wisdom, foresight
publice, publicly, at public expense, officially
publicus, -a, -um, public
pudet me, I am ashamed
pudor, -oris (*m*), shame
puella, -ae (*f*), girl
puer, -i (*m*), boy
pugio, -onis (*m*), dagger
pugna, -ae (*f*), fight, battle
pugno (1), to fight
pulcher, -chra, -chrum, beautiful
pulchritudo, -inis (*f*), beauty
pullarius, -i (*m*), chicken-keeper
pullus, -i (*m*), chicken
pulso (1), to beat, knock at
pulvinar, -aris (*n*), imperial seat (at games)
punio (4), to punish
pupa, -ae (*f*), doll
purus, -a, -um, clean, plain white
puto (1), to think

Q
quadringenti, -ae, -a, 400
quaestor, -oris (*m*), quaestor, treasurer, quartermaster
qualis, -is, -e, of what kind
quam! how!
quam, than
quam (+ *superlative*), as . . . as possible
quamquam, although
quando, when
quantum pecuniae, how much money
quasi, as if
-que, and
   -que . . . -que . . ., both . . . and . . .
queror (3), **questus sum,** to complain, whimper
qui, quae, quod, who
quidam, quaedam, quoddam, a certain
quidem, indeed
   ne . . . quidem, not even
quies, -etis (*f*), peace, rest
quiesco (3), **quievi, quietum,** to rest, sleep

quingenti, -ae, -a, 500
quinque, five
quintus, -a, -um, fifth
quis, quis, quid, who, what
    ne quis, in case anyone
    si quis, if anyone
quo, whither, where . . . to
quod, because, that
quomodo, how
quoniam, since
quoque, also
quot, how many

R

raeda, -ae (*f*), carriage
raedarius, -i (*m*), coachman, driver
ramosus, -a, -um, having many branches
ramus, -i (*m*), branch
rapio (3), **-rapui, raptum,** to snatch, seize
rarus, -a, -um, thinly scattered, rare, intermittently
ratis, -is (*f*), raft
recedo (3), **-cessi, -cessum,** to go back, retreat
reciproco (1), to brandish
recito (1), to read aloud, recite
recognitio, -onis (*f*), recognition
recognosco (3), **-novi, -nitum,** to review, recall to mind, revise
recte, rightly (in moral sense)
rectus, -a, -um, straight, direct
recumbo (3), **-cubui,** to lie down
reddo (3), **-didi, -ditum,** to give back, return
redeo, -ire, -ii, -itum, to go back, return
redimo (3), **-emi, -emptum,** to buy back
reduco (3), **-duxi, -ductum,** to lead back, take back
refero, -ferre, rettuli, relatum, to bring back, take back
    pedem referre, to retreat, withdraw
reficio (3), **-feci, -fectum,** to rebuild, repair, refresh
refugio (3), **-fugi,** to flee back
regio, -onis (*f*), region, area
regnum, -i (*n*), kingdom
rego (3), **rexi, rectum,** to rule, command, direct
regredior (3), **-gressus sum,** to go back, return
religio, -onis (*f*), religious belief, scruple(s), respect for the gods
relinquo (3), **-liqui, -lictum,** to leave
reliquus, -a, -um, remaining, rest of
remaneo (2), **-mansi, -mansum,** to remain, stay behind
remitto (3), **-misi, -missum,** to send back
repello (3), **reppuli, repulsum,** to drive back, beat back
repente, suddenly
repeto (3), **-ivi, -itum,** to seek again, revive, renew
reperio (4), **repperi, repertum,** to find out, discover
reporto (1), to carry back, win (a victory)
reprehendo (3), **-hendi, -hensum,** to scold, reprimand
requiesco (3), **-quievi, -quietum,** to rest, find rest
requiro (3), **-quisivi, -quisitum,** to seek to know, ask
res, rei (*f*), thing, matter, affair, situation, story
    rem bene gerere, to be successful
    res adversae, adversity, difficult times
    res secundae, success, prosperous times
    res urbanae, city affairs
    re vera, really, in actual fact
resisto (3), **-stiti** (+ *dat.*), to resist
respicio (3), **-spexi, -spectum,** to look back, look round
respondeo (2), **-spondi, -sponsum,** to reply
respublica, reipublicae (*f*), the state
resto (1), **-stiti,** to stop, stand still
resurgo (3), **-surrexi, -surrectum,** to rise again

rete, -is (*n*), net
retiarius, -i (*m*), one who fights with a net
retineo (2), **-ui, -tentum,** to hold back
retraho (3), **-traxi, -tractum,** to drag back
retro, back, backwards
re vera, really, in actual fact
revereor (2), **-veritus sum,** to be afraid of, respect
revoco (1), to call back, recall
revolo (1), to fly back
rex, regis (*m*), king, ruler
Rhodanus, -i (*m*), River Rhône
rideo (2), **risi, risum,** to laugh
ridiculus, -a, -um, laughable, funny little
rigidus, -a, -um, stiff, inflexible, stern
ripa, -ae (*f*), bank (of river)
rivus, -i (*m*), river, stream
rixa, -ae (*f*), quarrel
rixor (1), to quarrel
rogo (1), to ask
Roma, -ae (*f*), Rome
Romanus, -a, -um, Roman
rosa, -ae (*f*), rose
ruina, -ae (*f*), ruin, downfall, fall
rumpo (3), **rupi, ruptum,** to break, burst
rursum, again
rursus, again
rus, ruris (*n*), country, countryside

S

sacerdos, -dotis (*m*), priest
saepe, often
saevio (4) (+ *dat.*), to be fierce (towards), vent one's rage (upon)
saevus, -a, -um, fierce, savage
sagitta, -ae (*f*), arrow
sagittarius, -i (*m*), archer
sagulum, -i (*n*), military cloak
salus, -utis (*f*), safety
    saluti esse (+ *dat.*), to be a means of safety (to), be the salvation (of), save
saluto (1), to greet, hail, welcome, pay respects to
sanctus, -a, -um, holy
sanguis, -inis (*m*), blood
sapio (3), **sapivi,** to be wise
satis, enough
scala, -ae (*f*), ladder
scelestus, -a, -um, wicked
scelus, sceleris (*n*), crime, wickedness
scindo (3), **scidi, scissum,** to cut, tear open, split
scio (4), to know
scriba, -ae (*m*), clerk
scribo (3), **scripsi, scriptum,** to write, describe
scutum, -i (*n*), shield
se, himself, herself, itself, themselves
    secum, with him (her, it, them)
securus, -a, -um, untroubled
sed, but
sedeo (2), **sedi, sessum,** to sit
sedes, -is (*f*), seat
semisomnus, -a, -um, half-asleep
semper, always
senator, -oris (*m*), senator
senatus, -us (*m*), senate
senectus, -utis (*f*), old age
senesco (3), **senui,** to grow old, fail
senex, senis (*m*), old man
sentio (4), **sensi, sensum,** to feel, notice, realise
sepelio (4), **-ivi, sepultum,** to bury

septimus, -a, -um, seventh
sequor (3), **secutus sum,** to follow
serius, -a, -um, earnest, serious
sero, late
serpens, -entis (*m*), snake
servio (4) (+ *dat.*), to be a slave (to), serve
servo (1), to save, protect
servus, -i (*m*), slave
sex, six
si, if
sic, thus, in this way
sica, -ae (*f*), dagger
sicarius, -i (*m*), assassin, murderer
signifer, -i (*m*), standard-bearer
signum, -i (*n*), sign, signal, standard, statue
sileo (2), to be silent
silva, -ae (*f*), wood
similis, -is, -e, like, similar
simul, at the same time
simulac, as soon as
simulacrum, -i (*n*), image, likeness
simulo (1), to pretend
sine (+ *abl.*), without
sinister, -tra, -trum, left, on the left
sino (3), **sivi, situm,** to allow
sis = si vis, please
sisto (3), **stiti, statum,** to check, stop
situs, -a, -um, placed, situated
socius, -i (*m*), companion, ally, accomplice
sol, solis (*m*), sun
solarium, -i (*n*), sundial, balcony, flat top of a house
solea, -ae (*f*), sandal
soleo (2), **solitus sum,** to be accustomed
solitudo, -inis (*f*), loneliness, solitude, wilderness
sollicitus, -a, -um, anxious, worried
solus, -a, -um, alone
solvo (3), **solvi, solutum,** to loosen, free, set sail
somnus, -i (*m*), sleep
soror, -oris (*f*), sister
spatium, -i (*n*), space, interval
spectaculum, -i (*n*), spectacle, show
spectator, -oris (*m*), spectator
specto (1), to watch
spelunca, -ae (*f*), cave
spero (1), to hope
spes, spei (*f*), hope
spiro (1), to breathe
spondeo (2), **spopondi, sponsum,** to promise solemnly, pledge
sponsalia, -ium (*n.pl*), betrothal
statim, immediately
statua, -ae (*f*), statue
statuo (3), **-ui, statutum,** to set up
stipendium, -i (*n*), pay, a year's military service
sto (1), **steti, statum,** to stand
stola, -ae (*f*), stola, dress
stringo (3), **strinxi, strictum,** to draw (a sword)
studeo (2) (+ *dat.*), to study
studium, -i (*n*), zeal, eagerness, keenness
stultus, -a, -um, foolish
stupeo (2), to be stunned, be astounded
sub (+ *abl.*), under
subicio (3), **-ieci, -iectum,** to place under, subdue, subject
subito, suddenly
subsequor (3), **-secutus sum,** to follow closely
subsidio esse (+ *dat.*), to be a help (to), help, support
succido (3), **-cidi, -cisum,** to cut down, fell
suffragium, -i (*n*), vote
summus, -a, -um, the greatest, the top of

sumo (3), **sumpsi, sumptum,** to take, pick up, assume
superbe, proudly, haughtily
superbia, -ae (*f*), pride, arrogance
superbus, -a, -um, proud, arrogant
superi, -orum (*m.pl*), the gods above
superior, -oris, higher
superincidens, -entis, falling from above (on top of)
supero (1), to overcome, defeat
supplicium, -i (*n*), punishment
supra (+ *acc.*), above
supremus, -a, -um, highest, last, final
surgo, (3), **surrexi, surrectum,** to rise, get up
surripio (3), **-ripui, -reptum,** to steal
sustineo (2), **-tinui, -tentum,** to sustain, hold off
suus, -a, -um, his, her, its, their (own)
   sui, -orum (*m.pl*), his own men, family or friends

T
tabellarius, -i (*m*), courier
taberna, -ae (*f*), shop, cottage, inn
tablinum, -i (*n*), study
tabulae, -arum (*f.pl*), records
tabulatum, -i (*n*), floor, storey
taceo (2), to be silent
taeda, -ae (*f*), torch
talis, -is, -e, such, of such a kind
tam, so
   tam ... quam ..., as ... as ...
tamen, however
tamquam, as if, as though
tandem, at length, at last
tango (3), **tetigi, tactum,** to touch
tanti esse, to be so valuable
tantus, -a, -um, so great
taurus, -i (*m*), bull
telum, -i (*n*), weapon
temerarius, -a, -um, rash, reckless, bold
tempero (1), to refrain
tempestas, -atis (*f*), storm, weather
templum, -i (*n*), temple, area of sky marked off by augur
tempto (1), to try, put to the test
tempus, -oris (*n*), time
teneo (2), **-ui, tentum,** to hold, keep, confine
tensus, -a, -um, stretched
tenuis, -is, -e, thin, slender
tenuitas, -atis (*f*), thinness
tepidarium, -i (*n*), warm-room
tergeo (2), **tersi, tersum,** to dry, wipe
terminus, -i (*m*), boundary, limit, end
terra, -ae (*f*), earth, land
terreo (2), to frighten, terrify
terror, -oris (*m*), fear, terror
tertius, -a, -um, third
tessera, -ae (*f*), token, ticket
testudo, -inis (*f*), "tortoise", shelter
theatrum, -i (*n*), theatre
thermae, -arum (*f.pl*), baths
Tiberis, -is (*m*), Tiber
timeo (2), to fear, be afraid
toga, -ae (*f*), toga
   toga virilis, (plain white) toga worn by adult male
tot, so many
totus, -a, -um, all, whole of
trado (3), **-didi, -ditum,** to hand over
   tradunt, they say

traho (3), **traxi, tractum,** to drag
traicio (3), **-ieci, -iectum,** to take across, put across, cross
trano (1), to swim across
trans (+ *acc.*), across
transcurro (3), **-curri -cursum,** to run across
transeo, -ire, -ii, -itum, to go across, cross, pass through
transfero, -ferre, -tuli, -latum, to carry across
transfuga, -ae (*m*), deserter
transgredior (3), **-gressus sum,** to go across, cross
transnato (1), to swim across
trecenti, -ae, -a, 300
tremo (3), **-ui,** to tremble, quiver
tres, tres, tria, three
tribunal, -alis (*n*), platform (for magistrates)
tribunus, -i (*m*), tribune
tribus, -us (*f*), tribe, voting tribe
triclinium, -i (*n*), dining-room
tristis, -is, -e, sad
Troia, -ae (*f*), Troy
Troianus, -a, -um, Trojan
trucido (1), to slay, butcher
tu, you
tuba, -ae (*f*), trumpet
tum, then, at that moment
tunc, then, at that moment
tunica, -ae (*f*), tunic
turba, -ae (*f*), crowd
turris, -is (*f*), tower
tuus, -a, -um, your
tyrannus, -i (*m*), tyrant

U

ubi? where?
ubi, where, when
ultimus, -a, -um, last, latest
umbra, -ae (*f*), shadow, shade
umquam, ever
una, together
unda, -ae (*f*), wave
unde, where . . . from
undique, from all directions, everywhere
unguis, -is (*m*), talon
urbanus, -a, -um, of the city
   res urbanae, city affairs
urbs, urbis (*f*), city
urgeo (2), **ursi,** to press hard, put pressure on, urge, insist
uro (3), **ussi, ustum,** to burn, brand
usque ad, right up to
usui esse, to be of use
ut (+ *noun*), as, like
ut (+ *indicative*), when, as, how
ut (+ *subjunctive*), so that, that, to
uter, utra, utrum, which (of two)
uterque, utraque, utrumque, each, both
utilis, -is, -e, useful
utinam, I wish that, would that
utrum . . . an . . ., whether . . . or . . .
uxor, -oris (*f*), wife

V

vacuus, -a, -um, empty, empty-handed
vagus, -a, -um, wandering
valde, very, very much

vale! valete! Farewell! Goodbye!
valedico (3), **-dixi, -dictum,** to bid farewell
varius, -a, -um, different, various, varied, fickle
vasto (1), to lay waste, desolate
vastus, -a, -um, vast, huge, great
vehementer, violently, furiously, earnestly
velamen, -inis (*n*), shawl, veil
venatio, -onis (*f*), hunting
venia, -ae (*f*), pardon
venio (4), **veni, ventum,** to come
venor (1), to hunt
Venus, Veneris (*f*), Venus (goddess of love)
verbosus, -a, -um, talkative
verbum, -i (*n*), word
vereor (2), **veritus sum,** to fear
vero, truly
versus (+ *acc.*), turned towards, facing
versus, -us (*m*), verse, line (of poetry)
verto (3), **verti, versum,** to turn, change
verus, -a, -um, true
vesper, -eris (*m*), evening
vespera, -ae (*f*), evening
vestibulum, -i (*n*), entrance, passage
vestimenta, -orum (*n.pl*), clothes
vestis, -is (*f*), clothing
veto (1), **-ui, -itum,** to forbid
vetus, -eris, old
vexillum, -i (*n*), standard
vexo (1), to annoy, tease, harass
via, -ae (*f*), way, road
viator, -oris (*m*), traveller
vicinus, -a, -um, neighbouring
victor, -oris (*m*), victor, conqueror
victoria, -ae (*f*), victory
vicus, -i (*m*), village
video (2), **vidi, visum,** to see
videor (2), **visus sum,** to be seen, seem
vigilia, -ae (*f*), a watch
vigilo (1), to keep watch, lie awake
vilicus, -i (*m*), foreman, overseer
vilis, -is, -e, cheap, worthless
villa, -ae (*f*), country-house, house
vincio (4), **vinxi, vinctum,** to bind, tie up
vinco (3), **vici, victum,** to conquer, overcome
vir, viri (*m*), man
vires, (see vis)
viridis, -is, -e, green
virilis, -is, -e, belonging to a man, manly, adult
virtus, -utis (*f*), bravery, valour
vis (vim, vi) (*f*), force
   vires, -ium (*f.pl*), strength
visito (1), to go to see, visit
vita, -ae (*f*), life
vito (1), to avoid
vitupero (1), to criticise, disparage
vivo (3), **vixi, victum,** to live
vivus, -a, -um, living
voco (1), to call
volo, velle, volui, to wish, want
voluntas, -atis (*f*), wish, will, willingness
vos, you
vox, vocis (*f*), voice
   viva voce, orally
vulnero (1), to wound
vulnus, -eris (*n*), wound
vultus, -us (*m*), face, expression

SOLUTIONS

Unit IX, page 16

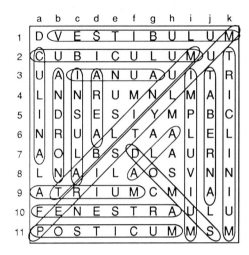

Unit X, page 30

The first number refers to the row, the second to the column, the third to the number of letters in the word. (Total possible points: 1079)

1. 4, 3, 7
2. 3, 13, 5
3. 4, 9, 9
4. 2, 17, 2
5. 3, 8, 4
6. 1, 6, 5
7. (2, 11, 2) (3, 14, 2) (4, 2, 2)
8. 1, 9, 3
9. 3, 11, 2
10. 3, 6, 5
11. 3, 12, 4
12. 4, 14, 3
13. (2, 6, 2) (2, 16, 2) (4, 16, 2)
14. 4, 9, 5
15. 3, 3, 5
16. 2, 13, 6
17. 4, 3, 4
18. 4, 16, 3
19. 2, 1, 7
20. (2, 1, 2) (3, 6, 2)
21. 2, 9, 4

22. 2, 3, 3
23. 3, 7, 4
24. (3, 15, 2) (4, 18, 2)
25. 2, 17, 2
26. 1, 3, 3
27. 3, 8, 6
28. 1, 10, 2
29. 3, 10, 4
30. 2, 8, 5
31. 1, 14, 6
32. 2, 18, 2
33. (1, 2, 2) (4, 17, 2)
34. 3, 12, 3
35. 1, 6, 6
36. 3, 1, 5
37. 1, 2, 3
38. 4, 1, 5
39. 2, 8, 8
40. 1, 2, 4
41. 2, 13, 5
42. 1, 16, 3

43. 3, 17, 2
44. 4, 5, 2
45. 2, 17, 3
46. 3, 13, 4
47. 1, 3, 5
48. 4, 1, 3
49. 3, 15, 5
50. 2, 13, 2
51. 1, 9, 2
52. 4, 1, 2
53. (2, 11, 2) (3, 14, 2) (4, 2, 2)
54. 3, 8, 3
55. 4, 8, 3
56. 1, 10, 6
57. 3, 10, 2
58. 3, 1, 4
59. 4, 1, 3
60. 1, 11, 5
61. 2, 6, 3
62. 1, 16, 4
63. 1, 1, 3

Unit XI, page 40

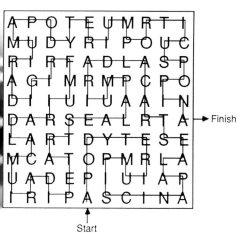

Start → Finish

Unit XII, page 50

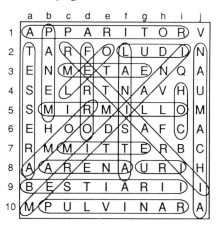

Unit XIII, page 62

Translations of Inscriptions (pages 58–9):

1 Sacred to the spirits of the dead. Ammonius, son of Damion, of the First Cohort of Spaniards, who served for 27 years. His heirs had this tomb erected.

2 Here lies L. Duccius Rufinus, son of Lucius, who belonged to the Voltinian tribe and came from Vienne. He was a standard-bearer in the Eighth Legion for 28 years.

3 Sacred to the spirits of the dead. Titus Flavius Candidus, from Ulpia Traiana, who served as a soldier for seven years in the Second Augustan Legion. He was 27 years old. His brother had this tomb erected.

4 Here lies Sextus Trebonius Proculus, son of Quintus, who belonged to the Fabian tribe and came from Beirut. He served for 13 years as chief clerk in the Fifteenth Legion which was dedicated to Apollo. He was 30 years old.

5 Sacred to the spirits of the dead. Calliste lived for 16 years, three months, six and a half hours. She was going to be wed on 15th October, but died four days before that. Her affectionate mother, Panathenais, erected this tomb to her dear daughter.

6 Sacred to the spirits of the dead. Here lies Leburna, manager of the troupe of actors, who lived for more or less 100 years. I died several times (on the stage), but never actually like this.

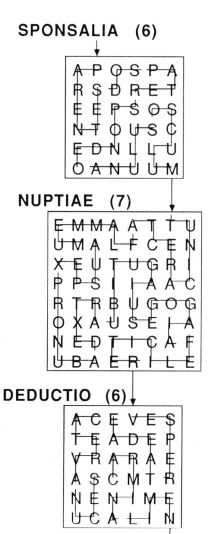

SPONSALIA (6)

NUPTIAE (7)

DEDUCTIO (6)

CAESAR
TACITUS
MARTIAL
CICERO
TERENCE
LIVY
VIRGIL
HORACE
GELLIUS
QUINTILIAN
JUVENAL
SENECA
PLINY
ENNIUS
OVID
TIBULLUS
PHAEDRUS
SUETONIUS

Quotations

AEQUAM MEMENTO REBUS IN
ARDUIS SERVARE MENTEM

HORACE

TEMPORA MUTANTUR—NOS
ET MUTAMUR IN ILLIS

ANONYMOUS

Reference Grid

C R Y M S
P I Q A G
E O B N V
T L D U H
J

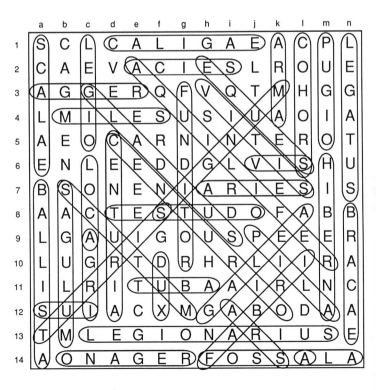